ON STAGE, OFF STAGE

MEMORIES OF A LIFETIME IN THE YIDDISH THEATRE
BY LUBA KADISON AND JOSEPH BULOFF

WITH IRVING GENN

HARVARD UNIVERSITY LIBRARY

Cambridge, Massachusetts

1992

Distributed by the Harvard University Press

Publication has been made possible
by the Sherman H. Starr Judaica
Library Publication Fund in the
Harvard College Library.

Library of Congress Cataloging-in-Publication Data

Kadison, Luba.
   On stage, off stage: memories of a lifetime in the Yiddish
theatre / by Luba Kadison and Joseph Buloff with Irving Genn.
      p.   cm.
   ISBN 0-674-63726-7 (pbk.: acid-free): $29.95
   1. Buloff, Joseph. 2. Kadison, Luba. 3. Theater, Yiddish—
History. 4. Vilna troupe. I. Buloff, Joseph. II. Genn, Irving.
III. Title.
PN3035.K26   1992
792'.028'0922—dc20
   [B]   92-40528
                                                        CIP

Text © 1992 by The President and Fellows of Harvard College.
Printed at the Office of the University Publisher.

DEDICATED

WITH LOVE TO OUR DAUGHTER

BARBARA

Preface

When the Joseph Buloff Yiddish Theatre Archive arrived at the Harvard College Library in 1986—the magnificent gift of Luba Kadison (Mrs. Joseph) Buloff and their daughter Barbara Buloff—the Harvard Library acquired a major resource for the study of the Yiddish theatre. Joseph and Luba Buloff were major figures on the Yiddish stage for more than half a century, and their remarkable archive documents their long and distinguished careers. Because of the centrality of the Buloffs to the development of Yiddish theatre, their archive is at the same time a treasure-trove of source material on the history of the Yiddish theatre.

The Buloff Archive is truly extraordinary in its comprehensive coverage and in the variety of materials contained therein. The archive includes hundreds of scripts translated and/or adapted by the Buloffs, as well as thousands of photographs, programs, posters, clippings and other theatrical memorabilia—all of which combine to provide a wealth of detailed information on the Yiddish theatre. The enormous potential of the Buloff Archive for scholarly research is enhanced by other resources available at Harvard that are particularly relevant: the Library's Judaica Collection (including its substantial Yiddish Collection) and the Library's Theatre Collection, and teaching and research programs in literature and in Jewish Studies. The recent establishment of a professorship in Yiddish literature adds another dimension to the role of the Buloff Archive at Harvard.

Included in the Buloff Archive were two fascinating works—*From the Old Marketplace*, a fictionalized account of his youth in Vilna by Joseph Buloff, and *On Stage, Off Stage*, a memoir of the Buloffs' career prepared by Luba Kadison Buloff. Joseph Buloff's work had appeared in its original Yiddish and in a Hebrew translation and in 1991 an English translation was published by the Harvard University Press, to considerable acclaim as a work of fiction of much literary merit. Luba Buloff's work is an autobiographical account of a remarkable theatrical team and her narrative thus provides the overall framework for the materials in the Buloff Archive. Therefore the Library proposed to publish this work with the addition of illustrations of selected items in the Buloff Archive, with captions provided by Luba Buloff. Until such time as a detailed catalog of the Buloff Archive is published, the present work, in addition to being a contribution to the history of the Yiddish theatre, can serve as an introduction to the kinds of materials to be found in the Buloff Archive. It is also a tribute to the Buloffs' keen sense of history that resulted in the creation of this extraordinary archive.

We wish to record the Library's gratitude to Luba Kadison Buloff and to Barbara Buloff for having entrusted to the Harvard Library this unique archive. The Buloff Archive will assist future generations of scholars in their study of this significant aspect of the Jewish cultural heritage and the vital and creative role played therein by Joseph and Luba Kadison Buloff.

Publication of this volume has been made possible by The Sherman H. Starr Judaica Library Publication Fund in the Harvard College Library. We are most grateful to Sherman H. Starr '46 for this generous support.

21 March 1992
Cambridge, Massachusetts

Charles Berlin
Lee M. Friedman Bibliographer in Judaica
in the Harvard College Library

Joseph Buloff and Luba Kadison Buloff, 1968.

ON STAGE, OFF STAGE

Memories of a Lifetime in the Yiddish Theatre

By Luba Kadison and Joseph Buloff

with Irving Genn

Introduction

What made me go back to remote memories of times past?

I am the last surviving member of the legendary Vilna Troupe, which for me was a school of life. Therefore, I felt a need to tell the story of this creative Yiddish theatre company. Even so, I hesitated for a long time.

I was eventually persuaded to begin writing by the enthusiasm of many good friends. At various times, in almost the same words, they all said to me: "You are the only one who can tell this story because you were present at the founding of the Vilna Troupe in 1916. You grew up in its theatrical atmosphere, as the daughter of its first director, Leib Kadison, and later as the wife of its most illustrious actor, Joseph Buloff. You took part in the opening of the Vilna Troupe's—and indeed the Jewish theatre's—most famous play, *The Dybbuk* by S. Ansky. Unless you write your memoirs, an important chapter in the history of Yiddish and European culture will be lost."

It was in response to such urgings that I undertook the difficult task of recording all that I could remember about the activities of the Vilna Troupe in the turbulent period between the two World Wars. I have also included later experiences of Buloff and myself in the theatre because, wherever we played—in Israel, Europe, South America or the United States—we always strove to follow the traditions of the Vilna Troupe, staging carefully rehearsed, ensemble productions of plays of literary merit in pure Yiddish.

To jolt my memory for relevant events in the past 60 years, I have had recourse to letters and writings left behind by my husband, Joseph Buloff. And it is in large part the color, warmth, imagery and humor of his own narrative style that this labor of love reflects. It is a privilege to be able to share the experiences of a life in the theatre of long ago. It is especially poignant for me to be able to share my personal experiences which included profound relations to family, fellow actors and friends of the Vilna Troupe. And of course it is a great joy to recount the splendid life and history with my partner, dearest friend and husband of sixty years, Joseph Buloff. My friend Irving Genn was instrumental in the translations of Yiddish texts and generally helpful in the compilation of the book. I want to express my heartfelt thanks to Irving Genn for his consistent support, loyalty and dedication. Our collaboration was always a pleasure and a journey together. I would like to express my gratitude to my dear friend Charles Berlin for his initiative in the publication of this book. With his effort and help he made it possible. Special thanks are due to Vicky Tamir, another dear friend, for editorial assistance..

Luba Kadison

Kovno

My story of the Vilna Troupe begins in the city of Kovno Lithuania, where strikes broke out in the year 1884. During one of them, a mob attacked and killed my grandfather, a factory manager they believed to be an informer. Soon it turned out that he had been falsely accused. That did not console his wife, who was left penniless with three small children, two boys and a girl.

For their sake, the young widow married an elderly man of uncompromisingly Orthodox views. A clash soon developed between him and Leib Kadison, the oldest boy, who grew up to become my father.

Leib, then about 9, was sent to *cheder* to study Torah and Talmud. He had the necessary intelligence for learning, but he was more interested in drawing pictures—caricatures of his teachers and fellow pupils and scenes from the Bible. He was enterprising too. He would demand that each of his schoolmates pay a groschen to look at his drawings, and with the earnings he bought pencils and crayons to draw more pictures. But one day Leib's stepfather discovered the drawings and, in a rage, shouting that a proper Jewish boy had to study the Talmud and not waste his time on foolishness, he tore up Leib's sketches and threw away his crayons. The boy never said a word. Early next morning, while the household was still asleep, he took his few possessions and left home. He went to a master signpainter and begged to be taken on as an apprentice.

The signpainter saw the boy would be an avid pupil and agreed to take him into his workshop. He taught Leib the trade and indeed became almost a father to him. Years later, Leib remembered that after his first day at work he smeared paint on his face and shirt, so that he could walk the streets with pride. Now he was a real painter, and it was the happiest day of his life.

He became an expert letterer in Yiddish and Russian. But that was only the first part of becoming a full-fledged signpainter. For the sake of semi-literate and illiterate customers, every sign in Kovno needed a picture of the trade. For instance, a shoemaker's sign had to have a drawing of a boot; a tailor needed a big cut-out of a pair of scissors. Leib became so imaginative, inventive and proficient that he was able to paint a huge sign for a baker of an angel distributing bread, challah and bagels from an overflowing sack. That masterpiece brought him his first recognition in his hometown.

Years passed, and the skinny apprentice grew up to become a sturdy man—ruggedly handsome, with a firm jaw, thick curly hair and strong features. Now it was time to find a girl and fall in love.

He met Chanah Mogel, a pretty brunette of 17, in a public garden where young men and women of modern views went to promenade, listen to band music and meet each other. She was from a good family that looked with disfavor upon a fatherless signpainter. Undeterred by her parents' disapproval, Chanah fell deeply in love and married Leib.

Kovno was prospering at the turn of the century; new businesses were opening, and there was enough work for two signpainting establishments. Therefore, Leib's old master wished him well when he opened his own workshop as a master signpainter.

Three children were born to Chanah and Leib Kadison: Paula in 1903, Itzhak in 1905 and I, Luba, in 1907.

Through hard work, Leib began to prosper as a sign maker and was able to add a sideline. A churchman who happened to see and admire his work engaged him to paint icons for churches and banners and vestments for Christian religious processions. Soon the workshop of this Jewish painter was filled with images of sad-eyed saints, hanging on the walls to dry. This was unheard of in the province of Kovno.

Not content with being a commercial signpainter and a religious artist, Leib Kadison acquired a hobby. He organized an amateur theatre group to perform plays by well-known Yiddish writers. In addition to producing, directing and acting, he designed and painted the scenery. He did that so well that the State Opera House of Kovno hired him as a scenic designer— a great achievement for a Kovno Jew and one in which the local Jewish community took due pride.

Father's workshop and the family's living quarters formed part of the same large apartment within a courtyard. There were several other families with businesses around the yard, including a pork butcher and a carpenter. The latter had a little boy named Misha. One morning, I saw the carpenter working on a little box in front of his shop. Misha had died, and his father was making a coffin. That first knowledge of death made a lasting impression on me.

The Kadison family, Kovno, 1912. Back row (left to right): Chanah and Leib; front row (left to right): Luba, Paula, Itzhak

Most of my other early memories are of happier scenes. When visitors came to our home, father would put me up on a chair and say, "Luba, recite something." I knew a few Yiddish songs that Father had taught me, and I willingly complied. That is how I got my first applause, which I greatly enjoyed.

The distinguished Yiddish playwright Peretz Hirschbein often visited our home when he came to Kovno. Once he took me on his knee and taught me a folksong about a poor naked child sleeping in an attic. I remember it to this day. The famous author Sholom Asch and other Yiddish writers also visited us in Kovno, attracted by my father's growing reputation as a man of the theatre and by my mother's generous hospitality within a truly Jewish home.

Chanah perceived her husband's public appearances as an actor as something beneath the dignity of a master craftsman and respected citizen. But she said little and busied herself with rearing her children and keeping house for her husband, his workers and apprentices.

Things were definitely looking up for our family. The older children were in elementary school. A tutor would come to teach us Hebrew. As father's business continued to grow, Mother was able to buy a piano for Paula, the musician in the family. I took piano lessons, too. We even had a maid, a peasant girl named Manka, who stayed with us for years through all our ups and downs.

Mother, Manka and we children spent the summer months in a small rented cottage at Katchergin, in the hinterland of Kovno, while Father continued to work in town and would join us on weekends. I remember the long, peaceful summer evenings on the screened porch, playing dominoes, singing songs or listening to stories.

One late-July evening 1914, as we were relaxing on the porch, we heard a crash. We rushed indoors and saw that a mirror had fallen from the wall and had shattered. Our landlady, an old peasant woman, crossed herself in panic and mumbled, "*Bozha moy*, God help us, something terrible is going to happen."

Later that night, we heard that Russia had declared war on Austria. The first World War had broken out. It changed everything.

World War 1: Vilna

The Jews of Kovno were among the first victims of the great war that was to destroy millions. For no apparent reason, the Russian general in command of the Polish-Lithuanian border area ordered all Jews to evacuate Kovno within 24 hours.

Hastily, my parents gathered together a few garments. Then Mother took Paula by the hand, Father led Itzhak, and Manka took me, and we all hurried to the railroad station. A huge crowd of terrified Jews, scrambling for places on the crowded trains, surrounded us. I became separated from my family and screamed in fright. Fortunately, some kind person pushed me through an open window of the train, where, miraculously, I landed in my mother's lap.

The train began a slow journey to Lithuania's principal city, Vilna. For the first and only time in my life, I saw my father crying.

We arrived in Vilna destitute. Father was in shock over the loss of his trade, his livelihood, his everything. It was now up to Mother to be the strong one in the family, and she rose to the challenge.

Within a week, she found an apartment at 11 Pagulanka Street—an apartment which a prosperous Jewish family fleeing from Vilna had abandoned leaving behind some of their furniture. It was a large flat on the fourth floor with many rooms, including an enormous living room, a dining room and a kitchen. We moved in.

Next, mother besieged government offices until a minister was persuaded to give her a permit to return briefly to Kovno. There she recovered our cooking utensils and furniture, including Paula's piano. She managed to load her treasure on a train full of cavalry horses, and brought it to Vilna. With our old furniture in place, 11 Pagulanka became a true home.

In Vilna, the German army had sent the Russians reeling and laid siege to the city. People were starving in the streets. The Jews lived in fear of Russian pogroms. Yet Mother managed to find food, mostly potatoes, for her family. But war touches a young child only remotely: As long as she is not actually under fire and has her family by her side, a little girl can almost ignore it.

After a year of siege, the Germans broke through the Russian defenses and captured Vilna. My recollection of this is dim and confused. I remember that we lay on the floor of our apartment, hiding under blankets, and that I heard the sound of hundreds of boots of Russian soldiers, running, fleeing.

The next morning, the beautifully uniformed German army marched in with bands and banners. It signalled an upturn of fortune for us.

Formation of the Vilna Troupe

To the Jews of Vilna, the German occupation was a liberation from czarist oppression and pogroms. The Germans of 1915 were not the Nazis of 1945, and the Jews were astonished to learn that there were Jewish officers and even a Hebrew chaplain in the German army.

Still, I recall that the Germans requisitioned all the brass utensils in Vilna. One morning, an efficient sergeant and several soldiers marched off with the pots and pans that my mother had so bravely salvaged from Kovno.

Even worse was the famine that stalked the streets of occupied Vilna. Squeezed by the blockade, the Germans began to seize foodstuffs in the occupied territories to ship back to their homeland. Soon, the population of Vilna was subsisting on coarse rations of black bread, eked out by whatever produce could be smuggled in from the countryside.

One cold winter morning when I was about 7, our maid Manka arose before dawn, because she had heard that a rare supply of white bread would be distributed. I begged to go with her. We stood on line for hours. I clutched ten kopecks in my stiff hand as I stamped my feet in loosely fitting boots to keep them from freezing. Finally, we reached the head of the bread line, where an official pushed my bread ration toward me. I opened my frozen fingers to pay, but, to my horror, the ten kopecks were gone. The official snatched back the bread and growled, "Move along."

I burst into tears. After picking up her bread, Manka tried to comfort me. "Never mind, Lubachka. You can have my share." I refused to be comforted and, still crying, let Manka take me home.

In the kitchen, I pulled off my boots, and the ten kopecks came tumbling out. They had slipped through my frozen fingers and down into the boot top during the long wait.

This was one of my few experiences of wartime deprivation. Somehow, Mother continued to keep her family from the worst ravages of hunger. I remember that a German officer who befriended Father and would bring us canned food and small cakes.

Now that I was old enough to enter elementary school, I needed a uniform: a brown dress with a black apron. Where could material for such a garment be found in wartime Vilna? Mother Chanah managed. She dyed a thin blanket, which a seamstress fashioned into the required uniform a brown colour with a black little aprois.

My father remained unemployed and downhearted. But the German occupation was to bring him a sudden change of fortune.

One day, to our apartment at 11 Pagulanka came two young amateur actors, Alexander Azro and Jacob Sherman, with a startling proposition. They had heard about Father's theatre work in Kovno and wanted his help in setting up a Yiddish dramatic company.

Leib was doubtful. How did they know that the Germans would permit it? Sherman and Azro reassured him. They had become friendly with a couple of German officers, Arnold Zweig and Hermann Struck, who were Jewish and had been writers in civilian life. Struck and Zweig were confident that they could persuade the military governor to permit and even support a Yiddish troupe. Because Vilna was full of amateur Jewish actors, there would be no trouble in gathering a talented company.

Stirred by the enthusiasm of Azro and Sherman and seeing a chance to resume the theatrical work he loved, Father agreed to join them as dramatic director. Right then and there, at 11 Pagulanda Street in occupied Vilna, the Federation of Yiddish Dramatic Actors (FADO) was formed. It was to become famous throughout eastern Europe as the Vilna Troupe.

Zweig and Struck kept their word. They went to the military governor and obtained permission for FADO to perform. An abandoned theatre, once the home of a circus, was secured.

I can only guess what arguments Zweig and Struck used to persuade the authorities. Perhaps they claimed that a Yiddish Theatre would steer the Jewish youth away from its interest in Russian culture. Or perhaps they argued that, since Yiddish is fairly close to German, soldiers in the German army would be able to understand the Yiddish plays and find diversion from the boredom of occupation duties. Whatever the arguments may have been, they proved so effective that the military government even supplied a sort of subsidy: a few sacks of potatoes.

Mother Chanah placed the potatoes in a small pantry in our apartment and guarded them as if they were jewels. Our huge living room was turned into a rehearsal hall as the new troupe began preparing its first play, *Der Landsmann (The Compatriot)* by Sholem Asch.

I remember that the actors ignored their hunger and were sustained mostly by youthful enthusiasm. Among them were Azro, handsome enough to be a matinee idol; Sonia Alomis, endowed with a musical voice and golden hair; Noah Nachbush, a unique character actor; Matthew Kowalski, the only professional in the company; Judith Laress, matronly and refined; Paula Walter, an engaging character actress; Tanin, a strong masculine type; Shneyer, a tailor by trade and a fine actor. They would gather around a small iron stove, from whose top Chanah would dole out the daily meal of the day: a baked potato for each. And all the while discussions without end would be held: What does an art theatre represent? What can one learn from Stanislavski and Vakhtangov? Can acting be taught? Which Yiddish dialect would be right for this theatre? Who is the greatest European playwright? The greatest Yiddish playwright?

Of course, most of these questions were never fully resolved, but the discussions helped to forge the ensemble style for which the Vilna Troupe was to become noted. Early, the Troupe decided that all the actors, regardless of their origin, would speak the same form of Yiddish: the literary Litvak style (avoiding, however, extreme regionalism that confuses the "s" and the "sh" sounds). Further, the Troupe collectively decided to build up a repertory of plays by the best Yiddish authors—I.L. Peretz, S. Ansky, Peretz Hirschbein and Sholem Asch—as well as by Russian and European playwrights, including Tolstoi, Andreyev and Sudermann.

With such a repertoire, the company could frequently perform the same plays and refine them to perfection. There were to be no stars; an actor who played the leading role in one performance might have a very small part the following night. Thus, in a time of famine and danger, the Vilna Troupe evolved an ideal for a literary, artistic theatre that would honor the Yiddish language and elevate the level of the Jewish public.

In preparing his first production according to such standards, Director Leib Kadison drove the young cast through forty rehearsals. An actress collapsed from starvation and exhaustion. She was revived with a glass of water and a hot potato, and the rehearsal continued.

On February 18, 1916, the Vilna Troupe presented the premiere of *Der Landsmann* by Sholem Asch on a splintered wooden stage, in front of the hard but crowded benches of the former circus theatre. The audience greeted the folksy comedy enthusiastically, and the Yiddish and German press ran favorable reviews. Thus was the Vilna Troupe auspiciously launched.

Leib Kadison, Kazimierz, 1918.

The Troupe followed *Der Landsmann* with *A Farvorfen Vinkel* (*A Remote Corner*) by our old, respected friend Peretz Hirschbein. It was an even greater success. In recognition of the Troupe's growing popularity, the German authorities turned the Vilna State Theatre over to them. Imagine, Jewish performers in control of a splendid municipal playhouse in the principal city of a Russian province. The Jews of Vilna were proud. The war had certainly turned the world upside down.

At about this time, Mordecai Mazo joined the company as managing director. He was a strong, good-looking man, a six-footer of athletic build and bearing who had been a teacher of gymnastics and fencing in Petrograd before the war had transplanted him to Vilna.

The success of the Vilna Troupe changed my mother's attitude toward the theatre. In Kovno, she had viewed playacting as something beneath the dignity of a rising businessman like her husband. But, in war-torn Vilna, she realized that FADO was not only a career for him but his salvation, and she threw herself into the enterprise. Chanah became the mother of the entire company.

We Kadison youngsters were inspired by the triumphs of the Vilna Troupe. My brother Itzhak formed a children's theatre in our apartment, where he staged the one-act play *Es Brent* (*Afire*) by I.L. Peretz.

For me, who was already appearing on stage with the Troupe, my brother's enterprise was no more than a game for children. My first part with the Vilna Troupe was that of a little boy in *Der Vilner Balebesil*. My sister Paula stayed out of the company, for she was already earning money as a pianist in cinemas and cafés.

Other plays that the Troupe presented in Vilna included *Di Puste Kretchme* (*The Vacant Inn*) by Hirschbein, *Days of Our Life* by L. Andreyev and *Der Dorfjung* by Leon Kobrin, as well as *Yankel Der Shmid* and *The Mother* by David Pinsky, *God of Vengeance* by Asch, *Shma Israel* and *The Eternal Wanderer* by Osip Dimov, *Shule Chaverim* (*School Friends*) by Ludwig Fulda, *Dolly* by Christansoff and *Miserere* by Iuskevitz.

Director Mazo capitalized on the growing reputation of the company by taking them on tour to Kovno, Bialystok, Grodno and other cities. In Kovno, the company presented *Jealousy* by Artsybashev and Sudermann's *Schemereing Shlacht*.

Luba Kadison playing a young boy in M. Arnstein's Der Vilner Balebesil, *Romania, ca. 1920, with the actresses (left to right) Judith Laress and Paula Walter.*

Back in Vilna, Mazo began working on another scheme. Realizing that war-weary Vilna had been played out, he moved heaven and earth to relocate the Troupe to the center of Jewish art and culture: Warsaw. And with the help of Zweig and Struck he succeeded.

Mother and the children were left behind in Vilna. Mother managed to keep us going by turning our apartment into a makeshift restaurant for writers and actors. We girls pitched in by waiting on tables after school. Itzhak helped with the accounts.

After a year, we received permission to join Father and the Troupe in Warsaw. We got away just in time, because shortly afterward the defeated Germans evacuated Vilna, and the city fell prey to contending armies in the Russian Civil War.

Buloff's Narrative: Civil War in Vilna

The Vilna that we left behind was subjected to terrible suffering. In the wake of the German retreat came occupation first by the Bolsheviks and then by the Polish Legion. The Polish invasion set off a pogrom against the Jewish population. Young Joseph Buloff, then at the threshold of an acting career, survived the horrors and later depicted them in a vivid, first-hand account.

Because every man's life is a chain, wrote Buloff, I start with the link that I picked up among the cauldrons in the Free Folk Soup Kitchen in the last days of the German occupation of the city of Vilna during World War I.

From the crack of dawn until halfway into the afternoon, thousands of men, women and children waited in endless lines for watery barley soup with only a smattering of potatoes or some scrawny carrots in it. Swathed in rags from head to toe, carrying pots, cans or tea kettles, they stood in line for hours, shivering in the cold Baltic air. Their faces drawn and emaciated, ration card in hand, they waited thus for a mere bit of food to get them through the day.

For me, there were no lines. The soup kitchen treated me as if I were an honored member of its family. The reason was that I had connections with smugglers.

Only about a third (or less) of the provisions of the soup kitchen came from the military government. The other two-thirds had to be supplied by smugglers who risked their lives to bring foodstuffs from the countryside into the beleaguered, starving city. I was the chief intermediary between the various bands of smugglers and the artibrator of their disputes. Therefore, I commanded respect whenever I walked into the soup kitchen.

Often, as I strode through the kitchen, I would notice an imposing, well-dressed woman who received her portion of soup without waiting on line or even showing a ration card. She was not exactly beautiful, but she did look attractive with her lustrous neatly combed black tresses and knowing hazel eyes behind an elegant pince-nez.

I inquired about her identity and learned that this was Mme. Sherman, the leading lady of the Yiddish Municipal Theatre that was located one flight above the Free Folk Soup Kitchen. During rehearsals, she and other performers would slip down into the kitchen to get a few spoonfuls of soup on the sly. They had to be careful to avoid the watchful eyes both of the supervisors and of the special blue-coated German police, as well as—and especially—the hungry crowds anxiously waiting in fear that there would be no more food by the time they reached the head of the line.

Once I had met Mme. Sherman (as well as her husband and the male lead Alchofsky, formerly of the Russian stage), the actors were no longer obliged to sneak into the soup kitchen. Thenceforth, ever morning before the kitchen opened, I would personally prepare a large pot of soup for them in exchange for the promise of a free ticket to the play they were staging, *Uriel Acosta*. Now I was a double smuggler: I spirited food away from the Germans and into the soup kitchen, and then from the kitchen to the actors.

I conducted this soup operation for several weeks but never got to see the play because, a few days before the opening, the Bolshevik army seized the city.

Under the new power, the famine worsened, for the smugglers were wiped out. The kitchen was transformed into a military barracks, the theatre into a meeting hall. As for me, I was reduced to one of the thousands that waited in long queues at potato distribution stations.

Joseph Buloff's parents, Benajmin (in Polish army uniform) and Sarah Bulkin (ca. 1914).

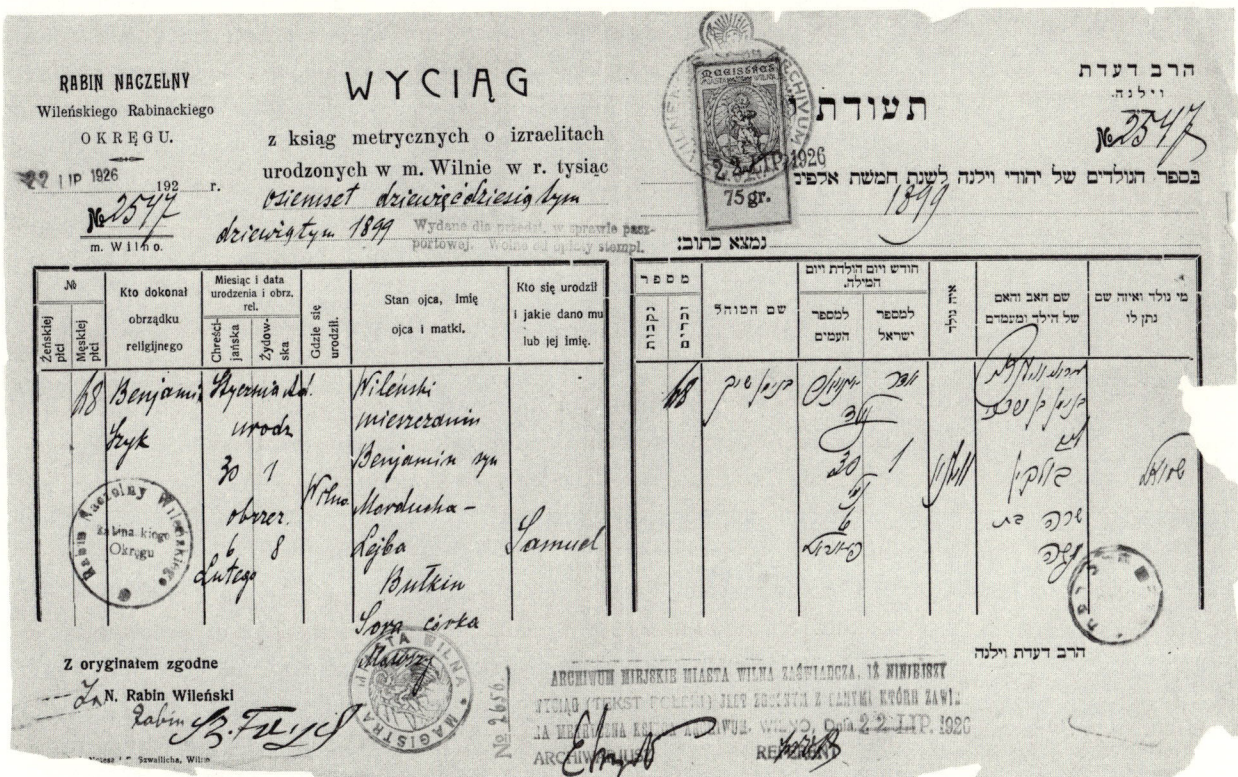

Joseph Buloff's birth certificate.

But gentle Mme. Sherman had not forgotten me, for one day she spotted me in a potato line and invited me to her home. There, on a table decked with a white tablecloth, I found a loaf of bread, a flask of wine, and a couple of fat herrings—all this at a time when people dying of hunger lay bloated in the streets.

At the table, Mme. Sherman introduced me in glowing terms to her other guest, the writer A. Veiter, praising my phenomenal memory. "Imagine," said she, "just from attending a few rehearsals of *Uriel Acosta*, this youngster virtually knows the script by heart."

I could not tell if Veiter was impressed. Elegantly dressed in a dark blue suit with a high stiff collar and tight cuffs, he spoke softly, using words sparingly and guardedly. On learning that he was a playwright, I eagerly attempted to engage him in conversation. But all I got were carefully chosen phrases. Who knows? He might have been more outgoing had he been able to foresee that one day I would play the lead in one of his plays and would try to invest my role with the memory of the well-groomed author in a blue suit who counted his every word.

I heard that Veiter was scheduled to deliver a lecture on the Yiddish writer I.L. Peretz, and though at the time I did not even know who Peretz was, I attended the lecture, driven perhaps by curiosity as to whether the taciturn speaker was capable of opening up and using full sentences.

In his discourse, Veiter drew a parallel between Peretz and the Polish poet Wyspianski. He lavished praise on Polish literature even as he recited whole stanzas of Polish poetry from memory. The sheer daring of the speaker overwhelmed me. In a time when terror reigned in Vilna and desperate battles were being waged between the Bolsheviks and the Polish Legion outside the city, he was not afraid to celebrate Polish literature. As I listened to him, I trembled in my seat as if in a fever.

After the lecture, Mme. Sherman and I went backstage to greet the speaker. There we met Arshansky, one of the founders of a new Yiddish State Theatre. When Mme. Sherman praised my good heart and wonderful memory, he embraced me and invited me to visit his theatre.

I saw a rehearsal in progress for Peretz Hirschbein's *Di Puste Kretchme* (*The Vacant Inn*), with the leading parts played by two young performers, Alexander Azro and Sonia Alomis, a husband and wife. From them I heard the name of the Vilna Troupe.

The Troupe had just moved from Vilna to Warsaw. The actor Azro and the actress Alomis told me that musical bands, flowers and banquets had greeted the Vilna Troupe on its triumphant journey to Warsaw and that they themselves had been the objects of audience adulation in several plays presented in Warsaw, including *The Vacant Inn*. That left me wondering why, after such successes, the two wandering stars had exchanged a *Vacant Inn* in Warsaw for a vacant inn in Vilna.

The answer came from one of those theatre mice—neither performers nor members of the audience—who hang around backstage, hide in corners and store up every event, date and gossip tidbit involving showpeople. From one such mouse, I learned that the manager and producer of the Vilna Troupe, Mordecai Mazo, had fallen in love with the actress Alomis, a beautiful blonde with plenty of feminine charm and a lovely musical voice. The trouble was that fond as she was of Mazo, Alomis had been even more strongly drawn to another actor, Alexander Stein. But as the rivalry between producer and player had gone on for the hand of Alomis, another actor, Azro, had appeared on the horizon and snatched the prize from the two contending roosters. The lovers had fled the company and returned to Vilna.

I was much impressed by this romantic story, and Azro and Alomis gained new stature in my eyes. As for the Vilna Troupe, in my youthful mind it became enrobed by a romantic, misty veil.

On the recommendation of Mme. Sherman, I was enrolled in the Yiddish State Theatre and received a part in *Di Puste Kretchme*. Alomis, with whom I, too, quickly fell in love, played the part of the country girl Mata. Mine was the role of Mata's mute bridegroom, jealous of Itzhak the horse thief, whom Azro portrayed as he storms the wedding with his gang and steals my bride from under the wedding canopy.

To my great joy, I was soon relieved of the non-speaking role as the mute groom. Since a stray bullet in the continuing street war had wounded the actor who was playing my father, I was given his part, replete with lines. Now I was to portray an elderly farmer with a long beard, who walked about with a chicken under his arm. On stage, I kept poking my hen to see if it was about to lay an egg, which caused the audience to roar with laughter, and that made me feel that I had arrived as an actor.

Forgotten was my unhappy childhood, as were my attempts to escape to the ends of the earth in a paper ship; forgotten also was my dream of becoming a famous violinist with a cigarbox fiddle, as were my arguments with God. Indeed forgotten for the moment were my real sorrows: my father's disappearance, the disasters of war, all the anger and Jealousy I had experienced. It seemed to me that the laughter and applause and excitement of the theatre had truly elevated me to the top of the world. And I found all that, and my pure love for the beautiful Alomis, in my first play.

But one night a bombardment shook the theatre. Audience and players fled and hid. In the streets, fighting and shooting broke out. At the railroad station, a long freight train had unexpectedly arrived, and when the cars' doors opened, Polish Legionnaires sprang out with fixed bayonets. Nobody knew how they had managed this Trojan horse stratagem. It worked, however, and the Poles captured Vilna that night.

One quarter of the Jewish population was slain, one quarter fled, and the rest fell victim to pogroms. The Yiddish State Theatre vanished in smoke, while most of the actors were left hiding in cellars or alleyways. Along with others, I fled into the hills.

Thus ended Chapter One of my theatrical career. A long time would elapse before fate could mend the broken chain that would lead me to the Vilna Troupe.

In the meantime, I led the life of a refugee on the war-torn Polish-Lithuanian border, surviving on potatoes or potato peels, and dodging flying bullets or whistling shells. One day, as I was climbing up the hills, I happened to run into another of the so-called theatre mice, who gave me news about gentle Mme. Sherman. He began by saying that on that terrible night the Legionnaires had seized the writer Veiter in his bed and dragged him half-naked into the street. Down on his knees, he had recited Wyspianski's poems in the hope of thus fending off bullets aimed at his head. The mouse then added that when Veiter was pulled out of his bed, Mme. Sherman ran after him in her nightgown and was severely wounded as she threw herself before the guns to protect him.

Another statement of dubious veracity followed: When the last performance of *The Vacant Inn* was disrupted by flying bullets, all the actors except me had allegedly run to save their womenfolk. As for me, I had grabbed my chicken and fled with it in hand. True or false, it felt good to hear again about Hirschbein's *Vacant Inn*, now vanished, abandoned, lost.

But more than my play had disappeared. The whole countryside was in the grip of civil war. It was not a conventional war, with positions and a strategic plan. Battles raged on the front, in the rear, on all sides. The city of Vilna was in the hands of the Poles, but the villages around it were held by the Bolsheviks. White Russian armies, each named for a general, battled the Bolsheviks, the Polish Legion and each other. Hamlets and villages changed hands countless times. One day the Poles held a village; the next day the Red Army captured it; then came the Whites. The cycle repeated itself over and over again, until the village became a giant cemetery without tombstones.

I managed to find shelter in a small village in no-man's land. Neither side was able to capture it, but it was under constant fire. Under a hail of shells, life went on. A peasant held a wedding for his daughter. A Jew held a circumcision ceremony for his new son. In the market place, trade continued—a shirt for a potato, a pair of pants for a head of cabbage. To facilitate commerce, there appeared a new scrip money system: Buyers and sellers exchanged pieces of paper signed and validated by the local priest or rabbi.

From all this, I learned that no fire can burn out the soul of man so long as the body holds together. While the stomach receives some food and a bit of courage, the soul survives. Besides, I had my memories of triumph on the stage in *The Vacant Inn* to sustain me.

At night, we refugees huddled together to discuss our plight. There were pessimists and there were optimists. Some said that we should go east to Russia, others proposed that we go west to Germany. A few even suggested France.

I knew that I was not fit for Red Russia. Nor was I interested in Germany or France. My destiny, I felt, was defined by the world I had found in *The Vacant Inn*. I remained in hiding in the village until I learned that the Poles had gained the upper hand and had restored a modicum of peace. Then I returned to Vilna.

Buloff's Narrative: Kompaneyetz

I had hardly been home a week when I received a message from the actor Alexander Stein. I rushed to his apartment. He opened the door and greeted me with, "Where have you been? I have been searching for you for weeks. Come in and get acquainted."

In the apartment I met an imposing character with a bluish-red nose, a thick underlip and a huge belly. "This is Kompaneyetz, a big producer of Yiddish Theatre in Lodz," said Stein.

"Pleased to meet you," muttered Kompaneyetz, holding out his hand. But before I could clasp it, he withdrew his hand, hastily excused himself and left the room.

"He has bladder trouble, has to go to the bathroom every few minutes," Stein explained. "But listen, I want you to read your crazy Jeanton Chantilly Delacroix monologue for him."

As soon as Kompaneyetz returned, still buttoning his trousers, I began reciting. He stopped me.

"That's Russian. Don't need it. Can you do Yiddish?"

"Sure. I know the entire *Vacant Inn* play," said I.

"What's *The Vacant Inn*? Never heard of it," Kompaneyetz confessed. "But never mind. It's not important. Just tell me, are you really a Vilner?"

"Sure."

"Native born?"

"What else?"

"Good. I am hiring you for the Vilna Troupe. Come to my hotel tomorrow morning, and we will make a contract."

The next morning I was at his door. A far-off voice told me to wait. Ten or fifteen minutes later, Kompaneyetz admitted me.

"Do you know who I am?" he asked.

"Certainly. Stein told me you are an important producer."

"Producer shmoducer. That's not the point. I am The Father. In times like these, a Jewish actor needs a father. He

Joseph Buloff, Vilna, 1912.

needs someone to give him a place to stay, a bed to sleep in, food to eat and a theatre to play in."

As I had no riposte, he continued, "My actors stay with me for twenty, thirty years. When they get married, I am the one who throws the wedding for them. When they die, I make the arrangements for a funeral."

I was about to walk out when he stopped me with, "Stein tells me that you either have no passport whatever or are holding a counterfeit one. Don't worry one way or the other, my boy! You now have found a father who will fix everything. Take a look!"

And Kompaneyetz showed me a photograph of himself shaking hands with General Pilsudski, the commander-in-chief of the Polish army. In addition, he pulled out and presented for scrutiny a silver cigarette case which bore the engraved name of the chief of police of Lodz, as well as a gold watch similarly inscribed by the governor of Warsaw.

"You won't find a better father," he assured me. "But I have to be sure that you are a true-blue Vilner. I must have Vilner. That is why I hired Alexander Stein, his brother Osik and that actor Avrom Morevsky. And that is the reason I am going to engage you, a genuine Vilna-born talent. With four big guns, Litvaks like you, I will show the Vilna Troupe wiseguys of Warsaw what Kompaneyetz can do. I will knock them down so hard they won't be able to get up even for the coming of the Messiah."

He then proceeded to inform me that the original Vilna Troupe had ruined the Yiddish Theatre. "The public is demanding Vilner. Just give them Vilner and only Vilner! Very well, if that's what it takes to fill the theatre, I will put real Vilner on the stage. How much?"

"How much what?"

"How much do you want per month?"

"I don't know," I muttered.

At this point, the producer abruptly ran out of the room and into the bathroom, but he continued speaking through the door: "What do you mean, you don't know?"

"Let me think about it," I shouted back.

To tell the truth, Kompaneyetz had confused me. On the one hand, he had called me a "big-gun Litvak" of the caliber of Stein and Morevsky. On the other, he had reminded me that I had neither a passport nor a job, nor even a father. Without so much as an audition, he was offering me a twenty-year presence on the stage as well as a bride at a future date and even a free funeral at the end. On top of all that, could I also ask for money?

Once again, Kompaneyetz's voice rang through the bathroom door, "I hear you are a teacher."

"I had a few pupils," I shouted back.

"And you have also been a bookkeeper."

"Yes. I handled a few accounts."

"A teacher and a bookkeeper. So you must be good with figures," he continued. "How much did you earn as a teacher? You know, an actor is also a teacher, though the hours are better. A two-hour performance in the evening, and all the rest is free time to eat, sleep and chase girls. Just tell me what you made as a teacher, and I will double it."

"I don't remember," said I. "I am no longer a teacher or a bookkeeper. I am now an actor. In *The Vacant Inn* I played the dumb bridegroom."

"So I heard. With me you won't play the groom. You will play the thief who steals the horse."

"Steals the bride," I corrected him.

"What's the difference?" he shrugged as he emerged from the bathroom. "A thief is a thief. I'll tell you what I'm going to do. For the part of the horse thief, I will pay you three times what you got for that of the groom. And transportation is free. You leave with me tonight. But you have to decide right away, because the train from Vilna to Lodz runs only three times a week, and tonight is the night. . . ."

I did not hear the rest, as I rushed home to pack.

The station was packed. Most of the cars had been requisitioned by either the White Russians or the Bolsheviks, as a result of which hundreds of desperate travelers were climbing over each other to reach the ticket window, waving money, pleading, cajoling.

But for Father Kompaneyetz this did not present a problem. He arrived at the station accompanied by a policeman, who proceeded to part the mob until he managed to squeeze us through and place us on the train to Lodz. Once inside, the producer led me by the hand and, all on his own, secured two seats. During the train ride to Poland, between frequent visits to the lavatory, he endlessly ranted about the Vilna Troupe.

Suddenly, he told me, "Go to the lavatory. Don't argue! Hurry up!"

I went to the lavatory, where I found three men who, like me, had no passports and were hiding from the conductor. Thus Kompaneyetz The Father got me from Vilna to Lodz.

On arriving in Lodz, my new father gave me a month's salary in advance and directed me to what he said was a cheap restaurant. But when I was presented with the bill, everything went black before my eyes. I discovered that my plate of soup and piece of meat amounted to half my salary. Everything began to loom darker still when the cheapest room I was able to find, a tiny garret owned by a seamstress, swallowed the rest of my monthly pay.

Completely insolvent, without a zloty to pay for breakfast, I charged back to my new father and accused him of swindling me. Kompaneyetz just patted me on the head and said, "A Vilner man of letters does not use such crude language. Let us call it a misunderstanding." Whereupon he tripled my salary, still barely enough to sustain me for a week.

When my fellow troupers Avrom Morevsky, Alexander Stein and Stein's brother Osik (now renamed Joseph Kamen) arrived, I hastened to tell them how Kompaneytz had swindled me. Since Stein was the one who had introduced me to the producer, he took it upon himself to straighten out my problem. Together we went to see Kompaneyetz, who greeted us warmly and offered us herrings and liquor. We finished the liquor flask and forgot why we had come. But Kompaneyetz reminded us by saying: "So it's only money! Mind you, if young Buloff is no better an actor than he is a bookkeeper, I am in deep trouble." And once again, he doubled my salary (by then tripled), which all the same still amounted to no more than a fifth of what my fellow actors were getting.

The next morning, I saw a huge poster in front of our theatre:

The True Vilner—Hooray for the Vilner!!

THE VILNA TROUPE
Morevsky   Kamen
Stein   Buloff

Three well-dressed young women were standing in front of the notice, apparently admiring it. To me it looked as if they were focusing on my name. My knees grew weak with excitement. When the ladies departed, I walked up to the notice and carefully eliminated a speck of dust that had landed on my name.

On entering the theatre, however, I heard wild shouting: "This is a fraud! The public is being deceived!" Morevsky and Stein were insisting that Kompaneyetz remove the poster.

Our producer tried to calm them down: "I don't understand you boys. You are from Vilna. You play literary pieces. You talk like the Vilner in *The Pintele Yid*. So why can't I call you Vilner?"

"But not *Troupe*," they argued.

"Four Vilner make up at least half a troupe, and if you teach the other actors to pronounce Yiddish Litvak style, we'll have a full, genuine Vilna Troupe."

Stein was not convinced. He took down the poster in front of the theatre and threatened that if all the other posters in Lodz were not similarly removed, he would resign.

So the offending posters came down. The new notice was even more to my liking, containing as it did just our names in big capital letters. But it, too, soon had to be replaced because Morevsky left the company. In his loud exchanges with our irresponsible producer, he had strained his vocal cords and become hoarse, with no sign of regaining his voice. Shortly thereafter, he returned to Vilna.

The next poster bore only three names—Stein, Kamen, Buloff—and it announced in large letters the forthcoming performance of The Eternal Wanderer by Osip Dimov. In it I played the Jew Shmul while Stein filled the part of the young student and Kamen that of the Russian policeman who proclaims the expulsion of all Jews from town.

Kompaneyetz himself played several minor parts, thus creating new difficulties, for in the middle of a scene, in the middle of even his own lines, he would run off the stage in need of the toilet. That necessitated improvisations by the rest of the cast until the character could re-enter. One of us would have to step forward into the footlights, to tell jokes or discuss the news of the day until Kompaneyetz, still buttoning his trousers, could reappear and *The Eternal Wanderer* could resume.

God bless the Lodz public! They put up with it all and even applauded, believing perhaps that this was how theatre was supposed to be.

One night, Kamen failed to materialize on stage as the Russian policeman. We realized that something had gone wrong—had he perhaps missed his cue? We were forced to improvise until the character finally showed up, not as the Russian policeman but as a Polish Legionnaire. Thereupon Stein, enraged by what he took to be a trick—and with his back to the audience—cursed and ordered him off the stage. But to our dismay, the Polish Legionnaire instead pulled off my beard and dragged me off the stage by the scruff of my neck. What I saw backstage was Kamen in his Russian policeman's costume, under arrest. I had been assaulted by a real Polish soldier.

It turned out that during our appearances in Lodz, the city of Vilna had been declared a part of Poland, and all young Vilner over the age of seventeen had been drafted into the Polish army. And Kamen, Stein and I were arrested for draft dodging.

All this was news to us. Worse yet, I had no passport and could not prove (nor did I even know) exactly how old I was. Stein was more fortunate in that he held an old Russian document exempting him from military service because of a touch of tuberculosis. Kamen, for his part, owned a counterfeit paper without the tuberculosis touch.

Kamen and I denied that we were Vilner. Yet the first "Hooray for the Vilner" poster, spread out as it was on a table at police headquarters, constituted irrefutable evidence that we were indeed sons of old Vilna. We were sternly informed that we would be handed over to the military in Vilna.

Stein's documented tuberculosis earned him his release. Consequently, the next theatre poster featured the name of only one actor—the sole remaining Vilner. But that notice, too, had to be taken down shortly, because Stein withdrew from the Troupe and went to Warsaw.

While my friend Kamen and I languished in one of the dark cells of the Lodz jail, Kompaneyetz proved to be indeed a father to us—a father who punishes with one hand and comforts with the other. True, he had gotten us into this mess in the first place, through his deceptive poster. But then he did not abandon us; three times a day he brought us food in jail, and he kept up our spirits with promises of an early release.

Finally, after three weeks of promises, Kompaneyetz produced two Polish passports for Kamen and me, replete with certification of advanced tuberculosis. We were released from prison and returned to the theatre. Our reward was a benefit gathering organized by the last of the old entrepreneurs in the peripatetic Jewish theatre. From the platform, Kompaneyetz extolled my friend and me as two proud Vilna actors honoring the Jewish people with their performances, in the purest of Yiddish, of dramatic pieces of literary and artistic value. He ended his speech with an appeal to the audience to drop contributions into a collection plate that had been placed on a table in front of the stage, flanked by two burning candles. Whether to honor us as Vilner or from pity for two alleged tuberculosis victims or simply because they had genuinely enjoyed our performances, the members of the public responded generously, and the collection plate was filled to overflowing.

Now we had both cash and passports in our pockets. We could go either to Warsaw or back home to Vilna. But how?

Under the prevailing wartime conditions of chaos, normal transportation, especially for Jews, was unthinkable. In the stinging November frost, hundreds—or perhaps even thousands—of people who jammed the Lodz railroad station would fight, kick, bite or trample one another to get on the first train that would finally arrive after hours of waiting. And when the train pulled out, scores of injured victims lay on the platform. At first, desperate passengers climbed up to the roof of the cars. But one time a train ran under a low bridge, and several heads were chopped off. After that, riding atop trains ceased.

For two days Joseph Kamen and I camped at the railroad station and fought to board a train. Finally, we went back to get help from Kompaneyetz.

We returned to the station with him, equipped with photographs, his silver cigarette case and his engraved gold watch. Without bothering to knock, Kompaneyetz boldly walked through a door marked No Admission and a few minutes later came out accompanied by two gendarmes.

The policemen pushed Kamen and me through the unruly mob onto a packed train's dirty third-class car, though ours were first-class tickets. But we were glad to be in anything on wheels. Through the dusty window panes we waved goodbye to our good father, whom we were now leaving before he had a chance to marry us off or provide us with a funeral. "I may never see him again," I thought. Later we heard that he had died suddenly in Lodz.

On the train the passengers stood pressed together like sardines. Angry voices kept blaming the Jews for the overcrowding. It was all the fault of dirty kikes who had seized the available trains for their own. That was the consensus.

"Instead of fighting the Bolsheviks, we should wipe out the Jews," a stylish lady sporting a hat with an ostrich plume proposed.

"What's the difference? The Jews and the Bolsheviks are one and the same," a worker in a sheepskin coat replied.

Kamen and I separated in the hope of blending more easily into the crowd. We stood stifled and sweating in the unventilated car while all around us curses against the Jews continued to rise in an ominous chorus.

Suddenly, a door was flung open, and a mighty wind blew in a drift of snow. An angry voice cried out, "Any Jews here?" Through the blowing snow, I was barely able to discern the uniforms of Polish soldiers. Several anti-Semites eagerly pointed to Kamen and me, and the soldiers grabbed us by the collar.

At a temperature below freezing, and as the train was rolling at a speed of 45 miles per hour, the soldiers ordered us off the train. Jumping would have meant death. We managed to climb out onto a narrow running board outside the car. By clinging to the window bars while balancing on the precarious ledge we avoided falling from the rushing train.

After ten minutes Kamen cried out to me, "I can't stand it. I'm going to jump."

"Don't do it," I called back over the roar of the wheels. "If you let go, you will be smashed to pieces."

"My legs won't hold me. My hands are frozen. I must let go."

"No, no, no! Please hold on! The train has to stop sometime soon. Please hold on, please, please, please!" I implored.

It looked as if we were doomed. Someone, however, had told the engineer about our plight, and the men mercifully halted at an unscheduled train stop. At that station, kind citizens carefully pulled us from the outside of the train, and we fell to the platform. Our legs could no longer hold us. For days we were unable to unclench our hands.

Barely recovered from our ordeal, we resumed our journey to Warsaw, where I was drafted into General Pilsudski's militia; yes, into the same Polish army that earlier had tried to kill me by throwing me off the train. Kamen managed to avoid the draft. Later, he would join me as a member of the Vilna Troupe and would do some fine acting.

Thus ends the fragment of Joseph Buloff's memoir, and I resume my own story of the Vilna Troupe in Warsaw.

Warsaw

By migrating to Warsaw in 1918, the Kadison family was spared the fate of the Jews of Vilna. A slowly dragging train carried mother and children to Poland. Baggage and bundles fell on our heads from the racks as the train started and halted, stalling and lurching its way to Warsaw.

It took two days to arrive at the main station, where the noisy, rushing crowds confused my young eyes and ears. But there stood Father, in the wintry light of the morning, waiting to welcome his family.

He led us to a vacant apartment to deposit our bundles and then took us to the home of friends who had prepared a special welcome meal for us. We hung our coats in an antechamber before entering the dining room to enjoy our first repast in Warsaw.

But disaster struck as we prepared to depart, and it followed us well into our own home. Someone had sneaked into our friends' antechamber and made off with Father's fur coat and Itzhak's overcoat. And when we returned to our apartment, we found all our baggage gone. On that very first day, we learned the full meaning of the Yiddish expression *Varshaver Gonovim* (Warsaw thieves).

Looking back, I can rationalize the thefts as symptoms of the prevailing desperation in the Polish capital. Hunger propelled people to grab whatever they could to survive the postwar turmoil.

Our losses depressed Father only momentarily. He had much to tell us about the Warsaw triumphs of the Vilna Troupe, which had taken over the Elysium Theatre and had added to the repertory brought from Vilna new plays such as *The Power of Darkness* by Tolstoi and *Di Neveyle* by Hirschbein. The new productions had been enthusiastically received by the Jewish audiences and press.

Journalisten Verein, the Jewish writers' club in Warsaw, was especially generous in its praise when it opened one of its reviews with the words, "FADO, you have won us over."

We moved into a two-room apartment at 28 Leshno Street in the Jewish quarter, not far from the Journalisten Verein, later made famous by the stories of Isaac Bashevis Singer. But we, five Kadisons and Manka, were not alone in the flat, for the family that had sublet it to us—a couple with a child and a spinster boarder—stayed on to share it with us. Six adults and four children crowded into two tiny rooms until the family of three moved out, to our great relief, but we never got rid of the boarder.

All the same, we were grateful that we had been reunited with both our father and the company. I resumed my juvenile acting career. In Maxim Gorki's *Lower Depths* I portrayed the shoemaker, and in Hirschbein's *Green Fields* little Avrom-Yankel.

Joseph Buloff's membership card in the Jewish actors' organization, Warsaw, 1922.

To the child that I was then, acting with the Vilna Troupe seemed as easy as drinking a glass of water. Acting came to me naturally. The Troupe was, after all, a family. We lived together, ate together, played together—what was there to be nervous about?

With Warsaw as its home base, the Vilna Troupe made tours of the provinces: Lodz, Cracow, Lemberg, Grodno, Belz. The reception Lodz accorded us was especially warm.

Our tours were organized by Mordecai Mazo, who negotiated with local producers for bookings, theatres and payments. If there were any profits, they were shared by the company members, with the higher percentages going to the leading players. But none was growing rich.

The Troupe stayed in second-rate hotels and ate at third-rate restaurants. I remember a friendly innkeeper in Lodz who warned us that the gefilte fish was too costly for our pocketbooks and offered us instead the sauce of the fish, which, when consumed with bread, made a passable meal.

When the box-office receipts were slim, the company suffered. Once, in a provincial town, we did not have enough money to turn on the lights in the theatre. But the resourceful Mazo solved the problem by activating the switchbox with a wire.

Mazo became the heart and soul of the Vilna Troupe. To him we were not a mere theatre group but an instrument for raising the Yiddish language and literature to high artistic standards.

During the early Warsaw period, beautiful Sonia Alomis was the great love of Mazo's life. However, she also had other suitors, Alexander Stein and Alexander Azro. Realizing that a woman must eventually choose one, she chose Azro, left the company at Lodz and eloped with him to Vilna.

As Joseph Buloff relayed it, Azro and Alomis founded their own company in Vilna. That was the first of many splits the original company was to undergo in the years ahead.

Mazo was distraught over the loss of Sonia Alomis. However, as a man of action, he searched Warsaw and found Miriam Orleska, a classic beauty who had been a teacher of Polish. She learned Yiddish and became our new leading lady. Soon Mazo and Orleska developed a close relationship and they stayed together for years. They never married, however, which was just as well, since Mazo was rumored to have a wife and two children in Petrograd.

About this time, Norvid and Shidlow, actors who had joined the Troupe in Warsaw, left for Moscow. Mazo filled the gap by adding to the company Kamen, Tarlow, Schick, Leah Naomi, and Miriam Videh. In Warsaw he also gained an actor of world caliber: Joseph Buloff.

First Meeting

After he was drafted, Joseph Buloff participated in Pilsudski's campaign that succeeded in repelling the Red Army under Trotsky at the gates of Warsaw. For this he was rewarded by being discharged without a zloty. Homeless and hungry, he roamed the streets of Warsaw until he resolved to turn to the Vilna Troupe, whose reputation had spread far and wide.

Buloff found the Elysium Theatre at 18 Korovo Street. He entered the darkened house, sat down at the rear of the orchestra section, and waited. After a while, Director Leib Kadison walked in.

"What are you doing here?" he asked.

"I am an actor," Buloff replied.

"Very good. And where do you live?"

"I don't live yet."

Kadison understood and asked the next, obvious question: "Have you eaten yet?"

"No."

"Then listen, young man. My wife Chanah is a great cook. Come tonight to my home at 28 Leshno. We will eat and then we will talk."

That evening when we heard a knock, I—a thirteen-year-old schoolgirl—went to open the door. There stood a young man in a torn jacket and tattered trousers with a shapeless cap pulled down over his left eye. I screamed.

That is how I met Joseph Buloff, the man who was to add luster to the Vilna Troupe and become my life's companion for sixty years.

Buloff was accepted into the Vilna Troupe despite his limited acting experience. After several walk-on parts, he was given a small speaking role in *Der Dorfjung*, in which he excelled through stage artifice of his own. In a group scene, for instance, featuring singing fishermen engaged in mending nets, Buloff, who played an apprentice with very little to do, instead of sitting idle, drew laughs and attention by taking out of his coat pockets chickpeas, throwing them into the air and then catching them in his mouth. The Troupe soon recognized his talent for invention and skills as an actor—which earned him increasingly better roles. His career as a major stage artist was launched.

The Dybbuk

Betrothed to each other by their fathers even before birth, Leah and Chanan meet by the power of destiny. Without a word between them, they fall in love. Leah's rich father breaks his vow and forces her to wed another. Chanan dies in despair, and Leah visits his grave. At her wedding, Leah violently rejects the groom, falls into a trance and begins to speak in a strange masculine voice. The soul of the dead Chanan has possessed her. A miracle-working rabbi exorcises Chanan's ghost. But Leah dies, and her soul is reunited with her true love beyond the grave.

Most readers will recognize the above as the bare outline of *The Dybbuk* by S. Ansky. It has been performed hundreds of times in a multitude of languages and styles all over the world. On one level *The Dybbuk* is a romantic story. On another it is a rich evocation of Jewish folklore. Some see it as a mystical affirmation of the power of love and justice.

It is certainly the best known play in the Yiddish repertory. Had the Vilna Troupe, FADO, accomplished nothing else in its three decades of existence, it would still have deserved to be honored and remembered for having discovered and premiered *The Dybbuk*. I, in my teens, was present at its inception.

One evening, my father said, "Luba, tomorrow we are going to Otvotsk to see the writer Ansky."

I was thrilled. Even though Father was earnestly interested in his children's education and progress, his work as a director, stage designer and actor left him little time to spend with us. Otvotsk, I knew, was a summer resort outside Warsaw, much favored by Jewish writers and intellectuals. And Father had told me that Ansky was a respected author and collector of Jewish folklore. I was therefore flattered that Father had chosen me, the youngest of the children, to accompany him on such an important mission for the company.

Dressed in my best white frock, with ribbons in my hair, I rode out with Father by train to Otvotsk. At a small summer cottage, Father introduced me to Ansky, a refined, soft-spoken elderly gentleman with a gray Vandyke beard and silvery hair. I sat quietly and listened.

Father first explained to Ansky that the Vilna Troupe was looking for a new play. Since Ansky had reportedly written a drama in Russian named *The Dybbuk*, which the great Stanislavski had considered for the Moscow Art Theatre but had ultimately rejected, would he agree to give the play to FADO?

Negotiations ensued, and in the end Ansky consented to the Troupe's acquisition of the play on condition that the Yiddish production be dignified and professionally staged. Then and there, he handed Father the script, and we took it back to Warsaw with great satisfaction. The memory of Ansky's gracious bearing and dignity has remained indelible in my mind.

Kadison and Mazo read, analyzed and discussed *The Dybbuk*. Then came the shocking news that Ansky had suddenly died.

At the funeral, which was attended by hundreds of Jewish actors, critics, dramatists and community leaders, Mazo delivered a eulogy. When he concluded with the vow that after the obligatory three-month period of mourning, the Vilna Troupe would honor the memory of the departed with a premier production of his masterpiece, *The Dybbuk*, a shiver of thrill and expectation ran through the crowd.

Spurred on by Mazo's pledge, our company worked feverishly on rehearsals. Leib Kadison outdid himself in his designs of somber, poetic sets. Miriam Orleska was cast as the doomed Leah. Alexander Stein, who had recently joined the Troupe, portrayed Chanan, while Joseph Buloff played the part of his friend and confidant. Father took the role of Leah's father, and I was Leah's young friend who greets the arriving bridegroom; the bridegroom was played by my brother, Itzhak. Avrum Morevsky, an actor with a unique personal style, portrayed the Meerypoler rabbi. Paula Walter was a sinister beggar crone, and Noah Nachbush played The Messenger whose pronouncements, in a haunting voice, express the underlying theme of the love betrayed by greed and injustice.

Finding a director for Ansky's play, however, proved a problem. While Father had previously directed almost all of our productions, he now realized that he lacked the Hassidic fervor necessary for the interpretation of this mystical tale. This time, a director steeped in the traditions of Orthodox Galician Jewry was required. At Morevsky's suggestion, David Hermann was engaged to direct *The Dybbuk*. He had been raised in a Hassidic household, which gave him the necessary understanding of the otherworldly spirit of the story and enabled him to project Ansky's vision into the production.

As Mazo had promised, exactly at *shloishim*—three months from the death of Ansky in 1920—the Vilna Troupe presented the world premiere of *The Dybbuk* at the Elysium Theatre in Warsaw. From the first chant of three Talmudists, proclaiming that the soul can rise to infinite heights and sink to the lowest depths, until the ecstatic cry of Leah, united in death with her lost love, the audience sat entranced. Then it rose in a tumultuous ovation.

The next morning, the press unanimously declared that the Vilna Troupe had brought something extraordinary to the Yiddish stage. The box office was so besieged that my mother had to become a cashier. Not only our regular audiences of modern Jews but also Hasidim in broad fur hats and long kaftans clamored for tickets. Polish intellectuals and actors, too, flocked to our theatre to view this unique product of the Jewish stage presented in the Polish capital of Warsaw.

Our actors basked in the glow of success. Special praise was lavished on Orleska for her touching portrayal of the star-crossed Leah. Later, some critics would observe that the part had marked her forever, that echoes of the haunted voice that had emanated from her Leah lingered on in her and surfaced in subsequent roles, almost as if a dybbuk had truly possessed her.

For me, too, *The Dybbuk* marked a kind of turning point in my young career. Once, at rehearsal, Director Hermann took notice of my deeply felt performance as Leah's girlfriend, and said to me, "Luba dear, you have ability. But you need training. You ought to enroll in drama school."

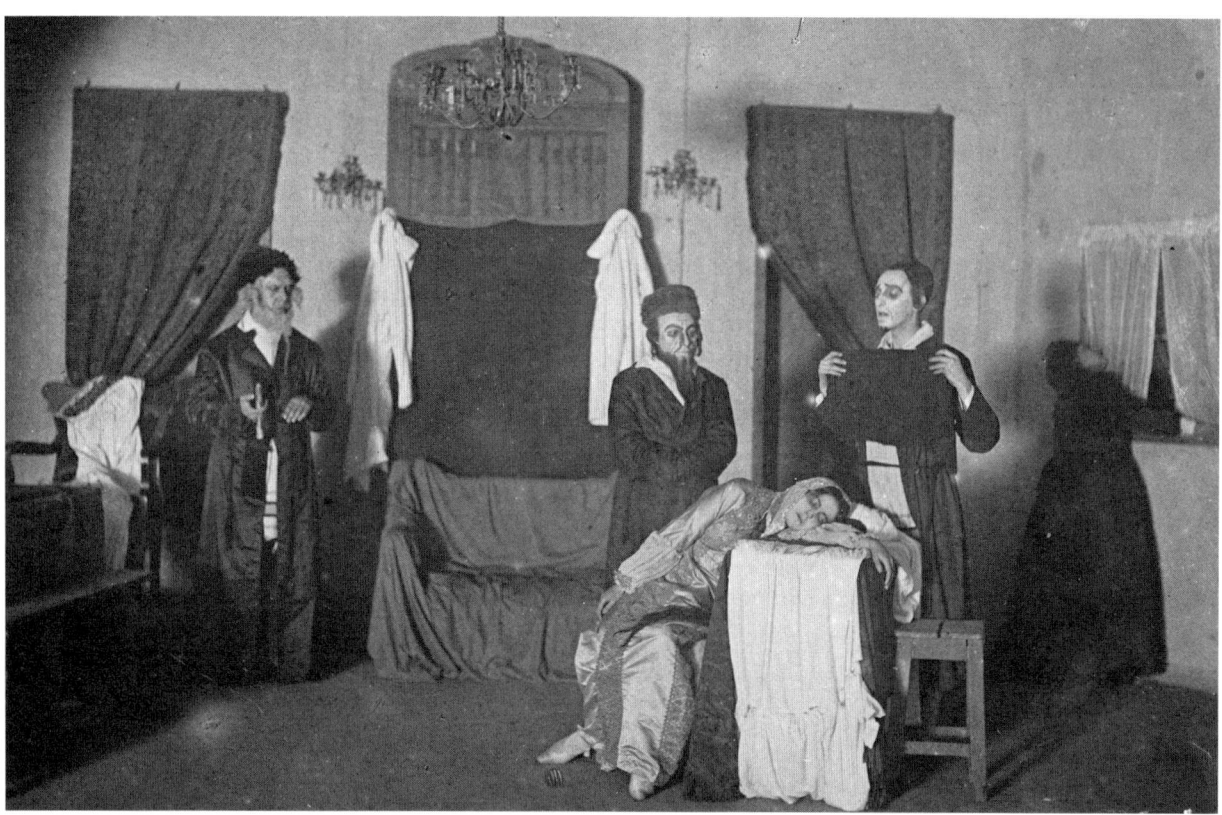

World premiere of S. Ansky's The Dybbuk, *Warsaw, 1920.*

Above: Left to right: Avrom Morevsky as the Rabbi, Noah Nachbush as the Messenger, Miriam Orleska as Leah, and Alexander Stein as Chanan. The set was by Leib Kadison.

Below: List of cast; from the program.

NA POGRANICZU DWÓCH ŚWIATÓW
(DER DYBUK)

Legenda dramatyczna w 3 aktach SZ. AN-SKIEGO.

OSOBY:

1 (Batłonym	(Abram Słobodski	
2 {	(Jakób Wajslic	
3	Józef Kamień	
	Samuel Szeftel	
Meszułach	(Noe. Nachbusz	
	(Szalom Tanin	
Chonon	(Aleksy Stein	
	(Józef Bułow	
Mejer, Szames	(Szalom Szac	
	(Szalom Tanin	
Henach (uczniowie	(Józef Bułow	
Oszer (jeszybotu	(Hewel Buzgan	
Sura Bas-Tojwim	Anna Braz	
Reb Sender Brinicer	(Jakób Wajslic	
	(Leib Kadison	
Leja, jego córka	(Mirjam Orleska	
	(Anna Braz	
Frade, jej niania	Judyta Lares	
Gitel (Koleżanki Leji	(Luba Kadison	
Basia (	(Pola Gołdhirsz	

Gość	Samuel Szeftel
Garbaty	Józef Bułow
Stara żebraczka	Jochwed Wajslic
Taniec śmierci	Pola Walter
Menasze, narzeczony Leji	Izaak Kowner
Reb Nachman, ojciec narzeczonego	(Leib Kadison (Józef Kamień
Reb Medel, nauczyciel narzeczonego	Hewel Buzgan
1 { Chasydzi 2 {	Samuel Szeftel
Reb Azryelkie Miropoler cadyk	(Abram Morewski (Mateusz Kowalski (Abram Słobodski
Michoel, gabe cadyka	Hewel Buzgan
Reb Szamszon, rabin miropolski	(Abram Słobodski (Szalom Kohn

Chasydzi, mechatonym, muzykanci, żebracy i t. d.

Wystawa: LEIB KADISON.

Sztuka odegrana będzie bez suflera.

"But there are no Yiddish drama schools in Warsaw," I replied.

"Then enroll in a Polish drama school," Hermann suggested, and pointed out that the best one was run by two famous Polish actresses, Visotska and Solska. His next advice was that I first learn a couple of Polish poems and then apply for admission and recite the poetry at my audition. Since I already knew Polish well, it was easy for me to memorize two poems: one by a popular woman poet, Konopnitska, and the other by Tuvim, a noted modernist poet. Then I went to the drama academy, where the school secretary interviewed me. With a pounding heart and the daring of a teenager, I declared, "I wish to become a Jewish actress, and have every intention of remaining on the Yiddish stage. But I know that I need formal instruction, so I am applying for admission to your school."

Visibly astonished by my audacity, the secretary nonetheless allowed me to audition. I put everything into my recital of the two Polish poems and was gratified when I was accepted.

I began to attend classes during the day and appeared in *The Dybbuk* and other plays at night. Visotska directed in dramatic scenes, while Solska taught poetry. There was also instruction in dancing, movement, interpretation and singing. I stayed at the academy for two years, where I received valuable training, learned classical and world literature, and acquired a lasting respect for the Polish theatre.

One day, Mme. Visotska took me aside and said, "I heard that you are appearing in that new play, *The Dybbuk*.

"Yes, Mme. Visotska, and I would be honored if you would care to attend."

The next evening, Visotska came to the Elysium. I sat beside her during the first act, translating the Yiddish dialogue in a whisper. For the second act I left my guest and went on stage, returning to resume my translation during the final act. At the closing curtain, Madame Visotska heartily applauded, embraced me and said the performance had been excellent. I basked in glory as I introduced her to the Yiddish cast backstage; I, the youngest member of the Vilna Troupe, had brought to it the great Visotska!

The Dybbuk continued to fill our Warsaw theatre to capacity, while the Azro-Alomis troupe took the play to Berlin and the Habimah produced a Hebrew *Dybbuk* in Moscow, under the direction of the famous Russian director Vakhtangov. Ansky's play was to become the Habimah's greatest vehicle. After moving to Palestine, Habimah performed *The Dybbuk* in a highly stylized manner, with the stress on the social conflict, in contrast to the folkloric, mystical interpretation by the Vilna Troupe.

Maurice Schwartz produced it in New York City. The Neighborhood Playhouse presented it in English. It was filmed in Yiddish in Poland. Pearl Lang did a dance version of it at the 92nd Street "Y."

To this day, seventy years after its Warsaw debut, Ansky's masterpiece continues to draw audiences. And as I write, it is being played in New York City by the Theatre of the Deaf. Paddy Chayefsky's modern version of it, *The Tenth Man*, ran on Broadway from 1959 to 1961 and closed only after 623 performances. Francine Prose built her novel *Hungry Hearts* around it, spinning a tale about an ingenue who played Leah in Buenos Aires and succumbed to the illusion that she was actually possessed by a dybbuk.

Luba Kadison as Leah in The Dybbuk, *Rumania, 1931.*

The novel resembles somewhat my own story, for I went on to play Leah in Buenos Aires (as well as in Bucharest), while Joseph Buloff doubled as Chanan and the rabbi. I also portrayed Leah in Maurice Schwartz's production that ran several seasons in the 1960's with the Yiddish Art Theatre in New York and on tour throughout the United States.

I remember best a performance as Leah in an all-star benefit for the Yiddish Art Theatre's actor Lazar Fried. Molly Picon played the beggar who spins in a death dance in the wedding scene. I told her how Paula Walter had interpreted the role in the original production, and Molly followed my advice, terrifying both Leah and the audience with her haunting cry, "Come dance with me, child, dance with me!"

As I played Leah, I never imagined that I myself was actually the haunted heroine. But I must admit to having experienced a transcendence, approximating Hamlet's pronouncement that "There are more things in heaven and earth . . . than are dreamt of in your philosophy."

The Vilna Troupe on Tour

The Dybuk was a financial success, and the Vilna Troupe was able to invest the profits in new productions. We presented the Biblical drama *Amnon and Tomar* by Asch, for which Leib Kadison painted elaborate sets and in which I appeared as an Egyptian dancer. M. Elkin directed both this and another Asch play, *Der Zindiker* (*The Sinner*). But neither play was well received.

The Troupe then returned to Ansky and produced his unfinished play *Tog un Nacht* (*Day and Night*), as completed by Alter Kacyzne, who was noted both as a writer and as a photographer of Jewish life. The play is set in a Polish shtetl menaced by the plague, which is blamed on secret witchcraft. In it, Joseph Buloff scored a personal triumph as a shamos who describes the witches' Sabbath in a harrowing monologue. Even though I was still a teenager, I took a cameo part as a mother grieving for her dead child, a dramatic role in which I symbolized, through stylized dance and song, all the mothers who had lost their children to the plague.

On a lighter note, we offered our audiences a charming comedy about a Jewish country family, *Green Fields*, by our old friend Peretz Hirschbein. My first part in that often-repeated play was as the little boy of the family. Paula Walter played the ingenue Tsenele, a role which I subsequently took over. We also presented *Shver Tsu Zein a Yid* (*Hard To Be A Jew*) by Sholom Aleichem.

With *The Dybbuk* and the other new plays, the Vilner made a triumphant tour of Poland and Galicia. As the wandering stars that we had become, we played Kishinev, Cracow, Lemberg, Chernowitz, Lodz, Belz. Our manager Mazo would arrange that a special train carry us, with all our sets and costumes, from town to town. Crowds greeted us at each station, while rival political factions (like the Bund and the Zionists) would compete for the honor of escorting the Vilna Troupe to the local theatre.

On the train, one car was set aside for the extras—young actors who had left behind their wives and families to join the tour without pay, just to be able to say that they had played with the Vilner. Mazo sustained them with watermelons and bread. Years later, Buloff would tell of his pleasure in joining the extras in their car to hear about their fantastic adventures in the Yiddish Theatre. He of course added to the extras' stories about wartime experiences and his stint with the legendary Kompaneyetz.

Because we Kadisons traveled as a family, we had to rent small apartments in each of the towns on the tour. These apartments became the center of the Troupe's social life, a place where the members could come together to discuss the latest productions, read their notices, complain about general conditions and exchange the latest gossip. Chanah Kadison, the unofficial mother of the company, made them all welcome.

Vilna Troupe poster listing repertory and members of the Troupe.

Almost forgotten was the terrible famine that the Troupe had suffered in earlier years. The times were now comparatively good, and food was no longer a problem in postwar Poland. With Mazo to look after them, the actors did not worry about tomorrow. If they had a little money left over at the end of the week, they would hand it to Mother with the request, "Hide it for us, Chanah!"

One day, Joseph Buloff came to her with a more serious problem. This is how he later recalled the incident:

In 1921 I should have been on top of the world. I was the leading man of the Vilna Troupe, learning something new from each performance and enjoying it immensely. We were touring Galicia in our own private train. In every town, cheering crowds met us at the station and carried us on their shoulders, like football heroes, all the way to the theatre.

Yet despite the adulation, all was not well with me. I continued to brood over the horrors to which I had been subjected as a youngster in the war. Vivid scenes of death and destruction invaded my mind and troubled my sleep. And one morning, it all came to a head.

I awoke in my hotel room in Lemberg, and as I looked in the mirror, I saw a bloody shell gazing back at me. I threw a sheet over the mirror, and the image faded. Trembling, I dressed and rushed out of the room. As I ran down the long hotel corridor, it seemed to me that from every one of forty doors, bony hands were reaching out to clutch me.

I hurried to the theatre and found there Chanah Kadison, who, with her warmth and understanding, was like a mother to us young actors. Sobbing and almost incoherent, I told her about my hallucinations. Was I losing my mind?

Chanah's face showed real concern. Yet she managed to calm me down with good advice.

"Listen to me," she said. "The most prominent doctor in Lemberg is a great fan of ours. Every night, no matter what we are playing, even if he has already seen the play three times, he is in the front row. I am sure he will help you."

Off I went across Lemberg to the office of Dr. Benedict. He was a short, bald man with kind eyes and an informal, jocular manner. When he heard that

Joseph Buloff on tour with the Vilna Troupe (1920's).

Buloff of the Vilna Troupe was calling on him, he canceled all his appointments and ushered me into his consulting room. There, for three solid hours, I talked to him about my experiences as a young man, between the ages of sixteen and twenty, as I had vainly searched for my soldier father in the midst of battles, revolution and civil war. I spoke of my struggles to survive as a conscript in different armies, of having been wounded and disfigured, and finally of my recent terrifying hallucinations. Never before had I told anyone all of this in such detail.

The doctor heard me out, and then he spoke: "Herr Buloff, I am not a specialist in these problems. Nevertheless, since the great war I have heard many stories like yours, and here is the advice I give those people. It often works. Make up your mind—now that you have managed to talk about the horrors—that by describing them you are eliminating them. Right now, in this very room, you have been born again, and all the suffering that you endured happened to someone else in another time. In other words, resolve to put it all behind you!"

I must have looked doubtful, because he continued, "I understand that next week the Vilna Troupe is going to Vienna. There is a doctor in that city who is doing new and wonderful work on problems like yours. He is a Jew and a man of culture, and as such will surely come to see the Vilna Troupe perform. I am certain that he will take you as a patient. His name? Let me see . . . Ah, yes, Dr. Sigmund Freud.

"However," Dr. Benedict went on, "I would still advise you first to try my prescription for mental health, because Dr. Freud not only charges his patients a fortune, but he makes them tell him dirty stories, too. In fact, there is a saying that before Freud we believed that a man is born with a small prong attached to him. After Freud, we must believe that a prong is born with a small man attached to it."

I found myself laughing. After thanking the doctor and offering to pay his fee—which he refused—I returned to the theatre and resolved to forget the past by fully immersing myself in my work. Thenceforth, whenever thoughts of war and desolation assailed me, I remembered Dr. Benedict's formula and reassured myself that I was reborn in 1920 and that the misfortunes of my former life no longer existed for me. And gradually it worked.

If Dr. Freud ever did come to see me act in Vienna, I certainly never heard about it. And of course I never consulted him. Too bad, for I might have occupied an interesting chapter in the great psychoanalyst's works—you know, something like "The Case of Joseph B.; War Neurosis Marking Infantile Father Fixation," or something else equally complex.

To be sure, I do not wish to disparage psychology or psychiatry. In fact, I have the greatest respect for those disciplines, especially since my daughter Barbara is a practicing psychotherapist in New York City. I can only hope she does her patients as much good as Dr. Benedict did me, through humor and simple practical advice.

Returning to my own memories of our tour of Poland and Galicia, I recall most vividly Belz, a small Galician town celebrated by the popular operetta tune, "Mein Shtetele Belz." Its unsophisticated inhabitants, eager to see *The Dybbuk*, would line up in front of the box office with their vegetables, eggs and chickens, to barter for theatre tickets. Another distinguishing feature of Belz were its mud puddles, so deep and sticky that I had to be carried to the theatre by young actors.

It would make a good story to say that Joseph Buloff carried me across a particularly nasty Belz mud hole, and that this is how we fell in love. But to be honest, I remember no such thing. To the best of my recollection, my first real conversation with Joe took place at a party in Lemberg, a gracious, cultured city where our fans consisted of "Doktor This" and "Advocat That." These Troupe aficionados used to throw marvelous parties for us. I was sitting in a corner in my

TRUPA WILEŃSKA
Zrzeszenie Żydowskich Artystów
Dramatycznych.

URIEL AKOSTA

Tragedja w 5-ciu aktach, K. Gutzkowa
przetłumaczył A· Morewski.

O s o b y :

Menasze van-der-Straten, bogaty
   kupiec Amsterdamu   Leib Kadison
Judyta, jego córka   Anna Braz
Ben Jochaj, jej narzeczony   Józef Kamen
De Sylwa, lekarz, jej wuj   Jakób Wajslic
Ben Akiba   Józef Bułow
Uriel Akosta   Aleksy Sztein
Estera, jego matka   Judyta Lares
Rubin } jego bracia   Szloma Kon
Joel }   M. Melman
Baruch Spinoza, chłopiec   Luba Kadison
De,Santos   Henri Tarło
Sługa Sylwego   Samuel Szeftel

Sługi, goście, tłum. Rzecz dzieje się w obrębie
miasta Amsterdamu w roku 1640.

ווילנער טרופע
פאַריין יידישע דראמאַטישע אַרטיסטן.

אוריאל אקאָסטא

טראַגעדיע אין 5 אקטן, פון קאַרל גוצקאוו
איבערזעצט פון א. מאָרעווסקי.

פ ע ר ו א נ ע ן :

מנשה וואַן-דער- סטראַטען,
   א רייכער סוחר אין אמסטערדאַם   לייב קאַדיסאָן
יהודית, זיין טאָכטער   חנה בראַז
בן-יוחאי, איר חתן   יוסף קאַמעו
דע סילווא, אן ארצט, איר פעטער   יעקב וויסליק
ר. בן עקיבא   יוסף בולאוו
אוריאל אקאסטא   אליהו שטיין
אסתר, זיין מוטער   יהודית לארעם
ראובן } זיינע ברידער   שלמה קאן
יואל }   מ. מעלמאן
ברוך ספינאזא, א יינגל   ליובע קאדיסאן
דע־סאנטאס   הענרי טארלא
סילווא'ס משרת   שמואל שעפטעל

שמשים, געסט, עולם.
איט און האנדלונג: אין און נעבן אמסטערראם, ציים 1640.

Drukarnia J. Fischera w Krakowie.

Program of the Vilna Troupe (Cracow, 1921?).

usual quiet way, when Buloff walked up to me and said in Russian, "Why are you so pensive, Luba?"

"I am not sad—just watching," I replied, also in Russian. We spent the rest of the evening in quiet conversation and discovered that we had much in common: dedication to the theatre, a love of Yiddish and Russian literature and, most important, an introspective bent.

That evening marked the beginning of a long courtship. Joseph first wooed me by reading me *Cyrano de Bergerac* in Russian translation. He would have made a great Cyrano, with his striking looks and flair for the romantic, and he charmed me with his rendition of the hopeless love of the noble but flawed French soldier-poet.

Buloff was not my first suitor. In Warsaw, my brother's many university friends openly courted me when they visited our home. In Lemberg, my parents favored a young doctor as a potential son-in-law. But I forgot all others once I realized that brilliant Joseph Buloff was genuinely interested in me. He failed, however, to impress Manka, the family maid and a second mama to me, who gloomily predicted, "You will have a miserable life if you accept him. He's not for you."

Heeding her well-intentioned warning, I told Joseph that I was too young for him and that we ought to break off the relationship. He took it hard.

Buloff's closest friend in the Troupe, Joseph Kamen, was married to sweet little Liza, who was a friend of mine. Buloff employed her as his messenger to pass on to me a love poem he had written for me. I still have it. He would also have her deliver to me pathetically fanciful messages like, "Riding on the train between Cracow and Lemberg, I watch with tearful eyes the telephone poles flashing by, and they seem to spell out L–U–B–A." What girl would not be touched? I took him back.

During our tour, Buloff wrote the following letter to Slobotsky, a Russian actor who learned Yiddish and joined the Vilna Troupe:

Cracow
May 1921

Dear Friend Slobotsky,
  Your last letter arrived in time. Together with wind-blown blossoms on the walls around our little hotel, posters are heralding the end of our season in Cracow. Soon we will be packing, to return to our dear Lemberg. On leaving Cracow, I have mixed feelings. From my window I can see the citadel on the hill, which harbors relics as ancient as the Paleolithic Age. Not far from the hill rise the gates of the Jewish ghetto.
  On Friday, the Jewish merchants close their little shops, and clad in long cloaks and great fur hats, they walk with measured steps homeward to greet the Sabbath. I see a pale youth with earlocks down to his shoulders—hands locked behind his back, head turned towards the heavens—passing by in rapt contemplation like a character from *The Dybbuk*.
  Our theatre is in the very heart of the ghetto. It is as poor and neglected as the ghetto itself. The street in front of the theatre is unpaved, muddy and full of little snot-nosed children. At the entrance to the theatre lies the public garbage heap, whose stench can be felt blocks away.
  The theatre scarcely holds 300 seats; the stage is barely large enough for five actors at a time. And yet I feel more at home in this playhouse than in Gimpel's theatre in Lemberg. At first, the Cracow audiences were quite cold, but gradually they warmed up to us until, just as we were about to proclaim success, a blow struck us. Now, our economic situation is at a critical low.
  Hungry mice can be fooled with a dried-up crust of bread. This is how Alexander Azro managed to mislead Paula Walter, Matthew Kowalsky and Noah Nachabush into leaving our company.
  Still, we continue to perform *Day and Night* (by Ansky) and to sleep until 2:00 in the afternoon.
  Slobotsky, you long to return to Russia. An understandable thing. You have difficulties with Yiddish, like Baratov.
  Speaking of Baratov, he once was a very handsome man. Now he is turning gray, and his eyes are dimming. Graceful in his movements despite his heavy build, he projects the image of an old lion who can still roar. He saw three of our presentations: *He Who Gets Slapped*, by Andreyev; *Gonovim*, by Bimko; and *Uriel Acosta*, by Gutzkow.

As the student in M. Artsybashev's Jealousy.

As Yonadav in S. Asch's Amnon and Tamar.

Joseph Buloff in various roles on tour with the Vilna Troupe, ca. 1920-1922.

As Count Mancini in L. Andreyev's He Who Gets Slapped.

As a thief in F. Bimko's Thieves.

As Chananye in S. Ansky's Day and Night.

I spent several evenings with Baratov in Cracow. One of his remarks delighted me. We were talking about drama, criticism, melodrama, literature, and he said: "We actors should not philosophize but feel. If I don't feel, I don't act. When I feel, I cry, and the audience shouts 'Bravo!' All else in the theatre is unimportant."

Buloff

Vienna

Young and in love in Vienna! We experienced it, for the Vilna Troupe traveled to the Austrian capital mainly on its reputation for *The Dybbuk.*

Hand in hand, Joseph and I strolled along and admired the theatres, parks, avenues and museums. We marveled at the Schonbrunn Palace. We drank coffee with *schlagrahm* and danced to Strauss waltzes in the Prater.

It was not all sightseeing, however. Since we were operating without a staff of dressers, I was asked to take care of all the extras' costumes for *The Dybbuk.* As soon as we arrived at the Roland Theatre in Vienna, I hastened to unpack a huge steamer trunk and to press a big pile of garments. Other members of the Troupe busied themselves with the hundreds of other tasks required for the preparation of a performance. We played *The Dybbuk, Shver Tsu Zein a Yid (Hard To Be A Jew), Green Fields* and *Tog un Nacht (Day and Night).*

Our old friends from the time of the occupation of Vilna, Arnold Zweig and Hermann Struck, welcomed us to Vienna and brought the renowned playwrights Richard Beer Hoffman and Arthur Schnitzler as well as the great tenor Leo Slezak to our performances.

The Vilna Troupe's production of Sholom Aleichem's Hard To Be a Jew, *Vienna, 1922. Left to right: Joseph Buloff, Leib Kadison, Paula Walter, Joseph Kamen, Luba Kadison.*

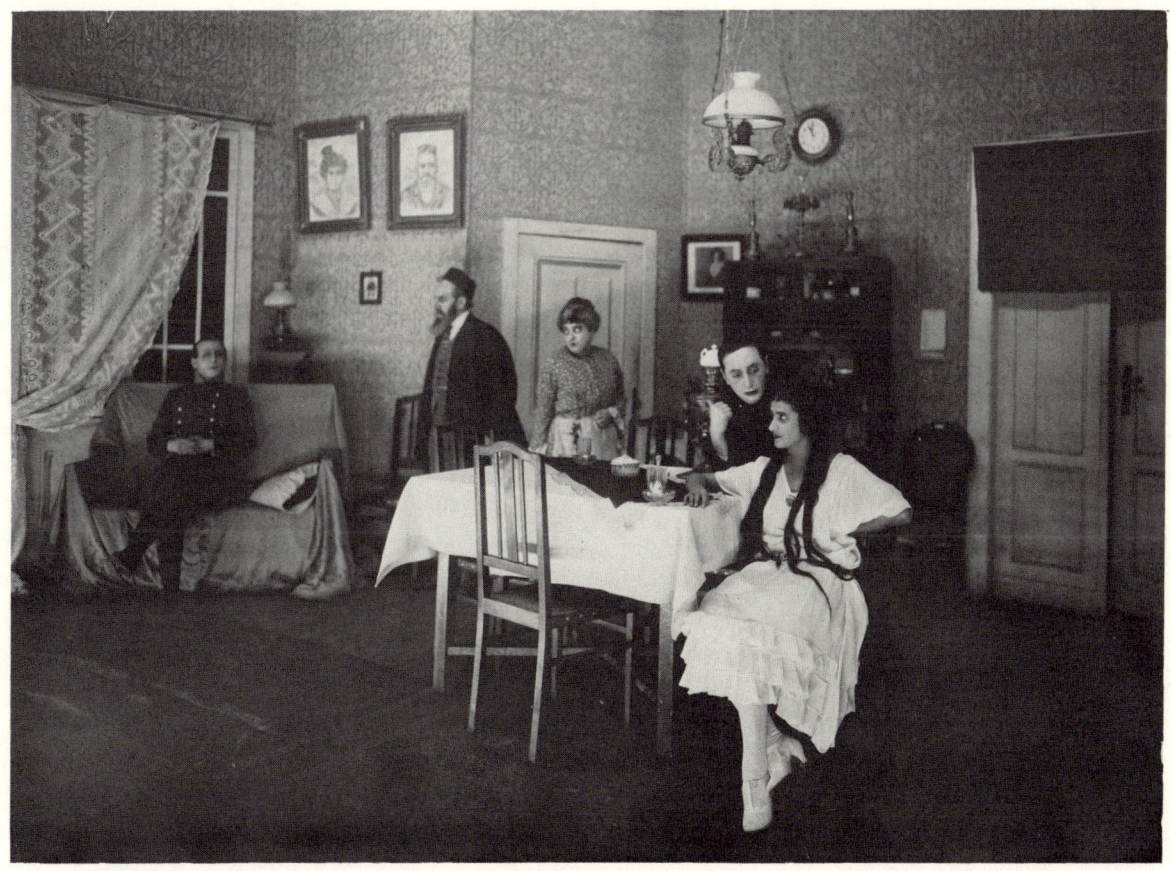

The most thrilling visit, however, was by Germany's pre-eminent director Max Reinhart, who, on the night that he sat in the audience for *The Dybbuk*, inspired us to give an outstanding performance. After the final curtain, Reinhart came backstage. We stood in awe before so distinguished a public persona, until Reinhart himself took the initiative by exclaiming in German: "This is not playacting! It is a religious rite." And he embraced each actor one by one.

Not all memories are equally pleasant. One day my parents received a telegram from Kacyzne, the writer who had completed Ansky's *Tog un Nacht*, urging them to return to Warsaw immediately in secret.

Mother undertook the journey by herself, since Father was performing with the Troupe. At the station she was met by Kacyzne, who told her that Itzhak was in hiding from the Polish police. Having remained behind in Warsaw, he had become involved in revolutionary activities and had set up a clandestine press in our apartment. Our unwelcome spinster boarder had betrayed him to the authorities, but he had been warned in time to take shelter with Katzizneh. Without delay, Mother and Kacyzne managed to smuggle Itzhak out of Poland to the Soviet Union on a forged passport. Father and Mother, and my sister Paula, saw him only once more; but I never saw my brother again.

I have yet another painful memory of that time. In 1922 as a side-tour from Vienna, Mazo booked us to perform *The Dybbuk* in Baden, even though we had been alerted that the anti-Semitic party Die Hakenkreutzer (Swastika) was planning a demonstration against the performance of a Yiddish play.

The theatre was packed with a disorderly mob. When the curtain rose, we began with the tremulous verse

> Wherefore, O wherefore
> Has the soul fallen
> From exalted heights
> To profoundest depths?

A strange stillness fell over the audience. Suddenly, someone in the audience began to cough. Others joined, amplifying the noise, until a veritable contagion of coughing afflicted the theatre. The actors continued to play. The coughers continued to cough, now adding hand-clapping and foot-stomping to create a deafening roar.

With our hearts pounding, we reached the point in the script where Hassidim break into song. The cast sang with a fervor that recalled the passion of martyrs. Then the anti-Semitic pre-Nazis broke into their own *Horst Wessel* song, and it was with that brutal anthem in our ears that we reached the end of the first act.

As the curtain came down, the local theatre manager warned us that the performance could not continue. Escorted by a convoy of police, the whole Troupe, still in costume—the men in long black coats and full beards—was led through the streets to the railroad station. Jeering crowds followed us. Some threw stones.

We had a warning, if not a foretaste, of the coming Holocaust. But we did not realize it at the time, hoping as we did that such evils would prove ephemeral, while the Yiddish language, literature and theatre, as indeed the Jews themselves, would endure.

From Baden we returned to the Roland Theatre in Vienna. Buloff's own memories of our Vienna season are contained in the following letter to a friend, a critic, actor and director.

Vienna
1923

Dear Veichert:

Barely arrived in Vienna, and at the railroad station itself the past returns—German-type bureaucracy, even if somewhat milder. They stop us with a complaint: Why are there only twenty of us and not twenty-one, as reported by Mazo? But in the end, though ours is a Jewish company, we are also theatre people, and theatre people are highly respected so we are admitted as twenty-one persons.

Good! We present *Green Fields*—and score a hit! *Fable shaftik shtik. Schpilen zei dan Yankele nach Dybbuk? Men zagt as zie zenen alle rabbiner und Talmudisten. Nicht wahr?*

Ironically, in Poland and Lithuania, they said that we were former professors and doctors. In Vienna, we are reputed as rabbis and Talmudic scholars.

Of the local leading personalities the noted playwright, Ber Hoffman, was the first to show interest in our theatre. He saw *The Dybbuk* twice, and the second time brought Max Reinhart with him. While the visit failed to augment our income, we were nevertheless enthusiastic: "Reinhart! Big news! Reinhart!"

He sat through the entire performance and then came backstage. An imposing man—Franz Josef sideburns, an elegant cane in hand. We were speechless with awe, yet greatly encouraged by his sympathy and friendliness. At the end he said with a smile: "Das ist nicht ein Schauspiel. Das ist ein Gottespiel." So much for my report on Reinhart's visit.

We came to Vienna fleeing from Warsaw as if from a fire, because of the bad acoustics in Kaminska's theatre. Now we are housed in a worse theatre, yet the problem here is not as grave, because here they don't understand our language anyhow. So, in a way, it is better that they can't hear us; besides, it doesn't seem to bother them.

We read in the Warsaw and Lemberg papers that our success is making us millionaires. That pleases me. As the saying goes, let our enemies burst with envy before they find out how empty our pockets really are. Still, from such joy, one can die of hunger.

The audiences we get here consist mainly of Polish and Ukrainian Jews on their way to Palestine: women with kerchiefs on their heads, youths in collarless shirts, all begging for free tickets. They also ask if we couldn't possibly play something more lively.

We do not hold Vienna, but Vienna holds us. We have no alternative.

We sit and wait. We repeat the performance of *Dorfjung* (*Countryboy*), eat cheap luncheons and read the foreign papers. We are told that the disguised second Kuni Lemel is amassing a fortune in London. But, they are probably just envious of us—the first, true Kuni Lemel.★

★ That is, Azro's second Vilna Troupe is in London, reportedly doing well, but probably envious of the original Vilna Troupe in Vienna.

Let us turn to more cheerful matters. The old Burgtheater of Vienna subsists on its tradition. Survivors of the Franz Josef era still attend its heavily stylized performances and forced, tear-jerking form of acting. I went there three times; it is like visiting a museum. I admired Sonnenthal's portrait and listened to old legends about the great star.

Reinhart's Deutsches Volkstheater is far more advanced; it has a number of lively Jewish actors. Oscar Bergie, one of the better actors, is Jewish, and fled persecution in Hungary. He is undoubtedly one of the strongest actors I have seen to date. In the same theatre, there is another Jew: the director himself, Reinhart. He came from Germany and settled recently in Vienna. Avrom Morevsky had a meeting with him. He found Reinhart unhappy with the present condition of the theatre.

I can tell you that we feel very small next to the great palaces of Vienna. And there are so many palaces in Vienna!

These days we are performing in a big concert hall. Never had a single Yiddish word been uttered there before. But we get more respect from Gentile Austrians than from the half-German Jews. German players come to our theatre and admire our work. Vienna's Caruso, Leo Slezak, and Arthur Schnitzler came to see our *Dybbuk*.

Buloff

Rumania

From Vienna we returned to Lemberg. The following season found us in Bucharest, Rumania.

Touring Rumania meant returning to the cradle of the Yiddish stage. For it was there, in 1876, that Avrom Goldfaden had started it all by presenting light comedies and musical skits in a wine cellar in Jassy. Now, in 1924, the Vilna Troupe was going to prove to the Rumanian public that the Yiddish Theatre had attained the level of art of some of the best theatres of Europe.

Our company incorporated new actors: Mr. and Mrs. Sandberg, Mr. and Mrs. Weislitz, Chanah Braz and Sheftel. Morevsky, Stein, Kamen and Buloff were the leading male performers; Orleska and Judith Laress, the female leads. I moved up to take on the role of Tsinele in *Green Fields*. Mazo and Leib Kadison served as chief directors.

Gone from the company were Paula Walter, Tanin, Noah Nachbush and Director David Hermann, who had joined the Azro-Alomis Vilna Troupe, now appearing in Western cities, including Berlin and London.

For the Rumanian repertoire we prepared *Uriel Acosta* by Gutzkow, with Morevsky in the title role. I played the young Spinoza. Buloff, not yet thirty, was

Luba Kadison (left) as the young Spinoza and Alexander Stein as Uriel Acosta in the Vilna Troupe production of K. Gutzkow's Uriel Acosta, *Bucharest, 1924.*

extremely impressive as the 100-year-old sage Ben Akiva. The Troupe also presented two plays by Andreyev, *He Who Gets Slapped* and *Days of Our Lives*.

Our theatre in Bucharest, the Zhitnetsa, was an open-air establishment and the permanent home of the Jewish theatre. I remember a band of Gypsies camping under our stage. Actors and Gypsies got along well. After all, we were all wanderers.

We found that Bucharest lived up to its reputation as the Paris of Eastern Europe—a beautiful city inhabited by light-hearted people. Eager to forget the war years, we indulged in good food, wine and entertainment.

The Rumanian public, Jews and Christians alike, received the Troupe enthusiastically. And word of our successes gradually spread westward, across the ocean to the great theatre metropolis New York, where Boris Tomashefsky was one of the old giants of Yiddish drama. As an actor, his name had become synonymous with bombast. Having acquired a huge Second Avenue theatre, he was now facing a challenge from a new force: Maurice Schwartz, founder of the Yiddish Art Theatre, whose dramatic productions were of a higher literacy and artistic caliber.

If art theatre was what the New York Jewish public wanted, Tomashefsky was determined to give it to them. He resolved to bring the Vilna Troupe, the foremost exponent of serious Yiddish Theatre in Europe, to the United States, and he undertook the journey to Rumania to persuade Mazo and Kadison.

My father was receptive to Tomashefsky's offer. My sister Paula had emigrated to America long before, was earning good money as the pianist at a popular Russian restaurant (the Kretchma on 14th Street), and wrote flowing letters from New York about the land of opportunity. But Mazo was opposed, because he felt that the Jewish-American public would not respond to our type of noncommercial theatre. He convinced the Troupe to remain in Rumania, where we were enjoying success and felt at home.

Tomashefsky was only temporarily defeated, however. From Bucharest he went to Berlin, where he easily persuaded the Azro-Alomis company to move on to America. Before departing, Azro dealt his most severe blow to the original Vilna Troupe by inviting Leib and Chanah Kadison to join him on the trip to America.

My father and mother were torn between reluctance to leave the Troupe, which had been their family for so many years, and a desire to try their luck and be reunited with Paula in America. Then again, joining their oldest daughter, Paula, meant leaving the younger one, me. For them, the solution to this problem seemed to lie in my marrying Joe, who had been my steady beau for some time. I would have a husband and protector, and my parents would be able to depart for America in peace.

Buloff and I were willing. Our life and work on the stage had brought us together, and the time was now ripe for matrimony. We agreed that the marriage would take place at Galatz, where we were scheduled to perform.

That was the ideal location for a wedding. The town is situated on a lake in one of the most beautiful parts of Rumania, where the king had a summer palace.

Thus, one afternoon we were officially united by the rabbi of Galatz under the traditional canopy, with the whole Troupe, dressed in their Sabbath best, present and shouting "mazel tov." The wedding was followed by a boat ride on the lake.

In the evening of that same day, we played *Green Fields*, Peretz Hirschbein's charming comedy about country life, in which a Jewish farmer hires the young scholar Levi Itzhak to teach the aleph beth and Talmud to his son. The farmer's vivacious daughter, Tsinele, also sits in, listens and learns how to write, even as she gets the pious young teacher to fall in love with her. In the final scene, Tsinele and Levi Itzhak are betrothed, and her father blesses the pair.

Since I had grown out of the little-brother role and was playing the romantic ingenue part of Tsinele, and Buloff was playing the teacher Levi Itzhak while my father took the role of Tsinele's father, it was my own father who pronounced the benediction over Joe and me on stage, before a rapt audience. For me that somehow made the stage wedding our true wedding. We stayed married for sixty years.

My parents left to join the second Vilna Troupe on its way to America, while Joe and I remained with the original Troupe in Europe. We had each other, and we had our work. But other problems of a professional nature troubled Joe.

The wedding of Luba Kadison and Joseph Buloff in Galatz, 1925, with the Vilna Troupe in attendance. Front row (left to right): Liza Stein; Leib Kadison; Joseph Buloff; Luba Kadison; Chanah Kadison; Alexander Stein; Mrs. Sandberg; second row: stagehand; Anna Braz; Jacob Weislitz; Yocheved Weislitz; Mr. Kremnitzer; Joseph Kamen; Mordecai Mazo; Miriam Orleska; Mr. Sandberg; Leo Halpern; Mrs. Sheftel; Mr. Sheftel; back row: stagehands.

Joesph Buloff on tour with the Vilna Troupe, Bucharest, 1920's: (top) as Levi Itzhak in P. Hirschbein's Green Fields; *(middle) as Ben Akiva in K. Gutzkow's* Uriel Acosta; *(bottom) as Chanan in S. Ansky's* The Dybbuk.

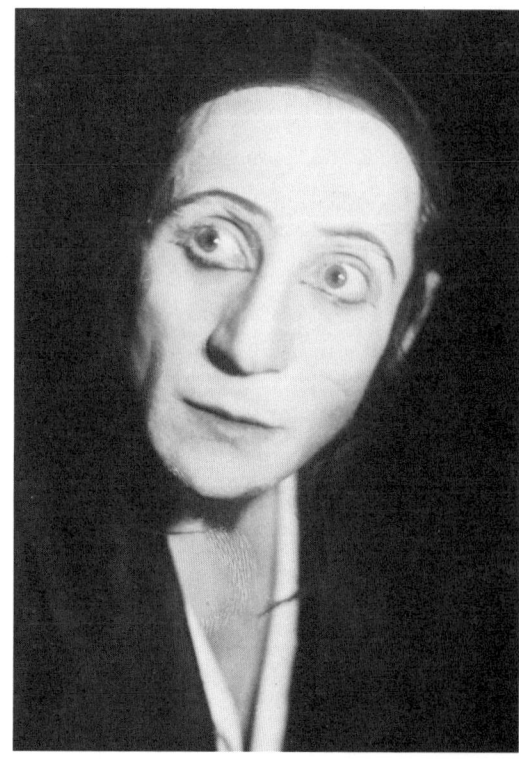

Looking for New Ways

Buloff had two reasons for being discontented. On the personal level, he felt he was not growing as an actor. He had early established himself as a popular favorite through his singular ability to win an audience from the moment he stepped on stage. Yet the Vilna Troupe was casting him mostly in supporting roles like that of the friend of Stein's Chanan in *The Dybbuk*. And in *Jealousy*, where Stein had the lead as a suspicious husband, Joe and I played comparatively minor parts as young students.

The more serious reason, however, for Buloff's disaffection with the company was artistic: He believed that it was falling behind the times. As an avid reader of theatrical books and journals, he was well aware that experimental drama was being staged in Berlin, Paris and Moscow. Under the influence of Vachtangov and Meyerhold, Shlomo Michoels was presenting Sholom Aleichem's *The Big Winner* in his Moscow Yiddish Art Theatre in a new, grotesquely stylized manner. And Cocteau in Paris and Toller and Sudermann in Germany were experimenting with surrealistic stage works. In Vienna, Buloff had seen for himself the innovative theatre of Reinhart.

Yet all the while, the Vilna Troupe continued to act in the realistic style of Stanislavski, with only *The Dybbuk* being interpreted in a mystical conception because of its spiritual, otherworldly theme.

Most of the other members of the Vilna Troupe—self-satisfied with their Bucharest successes—turned a deaf ear to Buloff's arguments in favor of an avant garde production. Thus blocked on both the personal and the artistic levels, he began to look around for a new affiliation.

He thought he had found one when an amateur group in Vienna offered him a free hand as star and director. Conscious that the Vilna Troupe, too, had started out as an amateur group, Buloff accepted, and, with high hopes, we departed for Vienna though we also had regrets about leaving the Troupe that had been the cradle of our theatrical careers.

The undertaking proved to be a disaster from the start. In Budapest we learned that our bags had been put on the wrong train, and we waited all night in a cold, deserted station for them to be returned. Then, when we arrived in Vienna, we discovered that our amateurs had promised more than they could deliver. They did not have the money either to rent a theatre or to mount a full-scale production. Soon we found ourselves doing scenes and readings in cellars before a handful of viewers.

We stayed at the Golden Adler Hotel, the same one that had accommodated the Vilna Troupe during its Vienna visit. But the hotel at that time had been filled with the gaiety and life of a functioning theatrical company, whereas now we found it to be lonely and cold as we saw ourselves running out of money. Undeniably, we had made a wrong move.

Vilna Troupe in Bucharest, 1925. Top center: Joseph Buloff; front row: Luba Kadison, 2nd from left; Mordecai Mazo, 3rd from left.

One evening, as well walked into the lobby of the Golden Adler after a long day of frustrating rehearsals, we found Mazo waiting for us. Even before we could get over our surprise, he simply said, "I have come to take you back to Bucharest."

Mazo must have had more than one reason for personally traveling to Vienna to secure our return. For one thing, word had reached him that we had been disappointed in Vienna, and he somehow felt responsible for the two kids of the Troupe. But more important was the fact that the critics and public of Bucharest had, in no uncertain terms, registered their sense of loss when the vital presence of Joseph Buloff was no longer felt and seen on the stage of the Zhitnetsa Theatre. And, last but not least, the Troupe was running out of plays and needed something new for its Jewish-Rumanian audiences.

Whatever the reasons, we were grateful for the rescue. But Buloff made firm conditions all the same, as evidenced by the following letter written about five years later to Nachum Meisel, a producer in Rumania:

New York
November 29, 1930

Dear Meisel:

I must begin with the year 1925: Mordecai Mazo came to Vienna to take Luba and me back to the Vilna Troupe, which we had left a short time before. We agreed to return with him to Bucharest. During the train ride through snow-covered Rumanian fields, Mazo and I reviewed my condition, which was that the Troupe shall be reorganized for the production of more artistic works. As a first step, it shall stage a play that I had long had in mind—*The Singer of His Sorrow* by Osip Dimov.

Mazo wondered why, given the number of available new worthwhile plays, I had fixed on what, in his opinion, was an insignificant, naive piece. I explained that my conception of the play was totally different from the text he knew from prior productions in Russian. I planned to use the script only as a vehicle toward a completely new piece that I had worked out in my mind. At first Mazo failed to grasp my point, but I at last convinced him that the play was to be reworked in order to fit the idea I wished to project.

At the home of Dr. Kepner in Bucharest—with the painter Reuven Rubin present—I read the play aloud and explained in full how it was to be changed. My audience responded with enthusiasm, and Rubin promptly embarked on the sketching of sets and costumes. I decided that for the time being, I had to be a writer, to roll up my sleeves and rework the script to fit it to my own conception.

Yours,
Buloff

The Singer of His Sorrow

The basic story that Buloff undertook to rewrite and restage is of a village musician and letter-writer, Yoshke Musicant, who loves the servant girl Shaineh. She is in love with Simonchek, her stern mistress's spendthrift son. When Simonchek shows up with a rich bride and her overbearing family, Shaineh is thrown into despair. Things seem to take a lighter turn when Yoshke wins a lottery and imagines that he can now wed Shaineh. But she tells him that she is going to have a baby by Simonchek, whom she still loves. In a most gallant manner, Yoshke manages to lose all his money to Simonchek in a card game in order to enable the playboy to wed Shaineh and give her unborn child a name. At the end, all the town beggars descend on Yoshke, strip him of his remaining possessions, and—as the curtain falls—leave him a broken man.

To play this simplistic script in a realistic style was as impossible in 1925 as it would be today. Instead, Buloff set out to present it as pure fantasy. Accordingly, he added a prologue, in which an old woman is about to narrate a story to her grandchild Rosalie, but suddenly the granny changes into Yoshke, and the main story begins. The audience thus is induced to view the action through the eyes of the child Rosalie. With her, it sees everything as larger and more colorful than real life.

The childlike vision was maintained throughout. In Buloff's production, the actress portraying an old chicken vendor mimicked and was costumed as a hen. A chimney sweep, black with soot from head to toe, made his entrances and exits

World premiere of O. Dimov's Singer of His Sorrow, *Bucharest, 1924. Left foreground: Joseph Buloff.*

Cântărețul tristeței sale

Tragi comedie în 3 acte, un prolog și un epilog de Osip Dymov. Pusa în scenă de I. Bulov

PERSOANELE

Bunică . . . . *.	Schaike, un coșar｜ . . . D-l *J. Ehrenkrantz*
Nepoată . . . . . . *.	Hodeș, o vânzătoare de păsări . D-na *Judith Lares*
Madam Lurie . . . D-na *I. Weislitz*	Mendel, un misit . . . . D-l *S. Natan*
Simiontschik . . . . D-l *Henry Tarlo*	
Roizale . . . . . . D-na *Liuba Kadison*	Un rabin . . . . D-l *I. Schönbaum*
Scheine . . . . . . D-ra *Anna Braz*	Un cerșetor mut . . . . *. .
Beril, un sacagiu . . D-l *Iacob Weislitz*	Un cerșetor . . . . . . D-l *Simi Weinstock*
Ioșke . . . . D-l *Iosef Bulov*	O cerșetoare . . . . . . D-ra *Sternitzka*

Mobilele și obiectele de Artă sunt furnizate de
Expoziția PASCU Str. Sf. Vineri, 15. Telefon 35-4

Mobile de Fer și Bronz
găsiți la Fabrica
GUTMAN MARCUS
Str. Sf. Apostol, 72 colț cu Calea Rahovei. Telefon 25-63

Program of Vilna Troupe's production of O. Dimov's Singer of His Sorrow, *Bucharest, 1924.*

through the stove. And all other characters similarly bore the exaggerated features of their respective occupations.

Reuven Rubin, later to become one of Israel's greatest painters, designed the sets and costumes in the bright primary colors of folk art. Buloff dazzled the audience both through his direction and in the dual role of the aged grandmother and youthful Yoshke, as he quickly switched from one to the other. As Yoshke, the village musician and writer of love letters, he struck a poetic, romantic chord that charmed the public night after night.

I played little Rosalie; Judith Laress turned herself into a chicken as the hen woman; Joseph Kamen portrayed Sheike, the chimney sweep; Anna Braz, Shaineh; Nathan, the cemetery salesman; and Weislitz played Yoshke's father, a humble water carrier.

Next to *The Dybbuk, Singer of His Sorrow* became the Troupe's greatest hit, for it brought something new to the Rumanian public: a theatre of fantasy and imagination.

Among the many who saw it more than once was the wealthy Rumanian Jew Wolf Lupescu. He praised it so highly to his daughter that she came to one of our performances, and, struck by the production's riveting novelty, spoke around it to her highly placed lover, who was so intrigued that he decided to see it himself.

Now, since Lupesco's daughter Magda was none other than the much-vaunted mistress of King Carol of Rumania, the Vilna Troupe received an order to present a command performance for His Majesty, his bodyguard and a few governmental officials. Our company of vagabonds had come a long way!

Mazo and Buloff ran about in search of cushioned chairs to spare our noble guests the discomfort of sitting on the Zhitnetsa Theatre's hard benches.

But when the time came for the curtain to rise on the special performance, Laress discovered that her long, feathered gloves for the costume of a hen woman had been misplaced. And the royal Rumanian party was forced to wait until a Jewish actress could find her gloves.

Apparently, the show was worth the wait, because the king and his courtiers applauded heartily, and the king presented Buloff with a bouquet and a ribbon bearing a complimentary inscription. A while later, on his visit to Rumania the king of Greece also attended one of our regular performances. It was common at the time for entertainers to boast that they had played "before the crowned heads of Europe," whether that was true or not. But for the Vilna Troupe that was unembellished fact—thanks to Buloff's *The Singer of His Sorrow*.

When the author of the original play, Osip Dimov, heard about our success, he exclaimed: "How marvelous! Who wrote it?"

Next came Buloff's production of *Sabbatai Zvi* by Jerzy Zulawski. Not only did he adapt and translate into Yiddish the Polish original, but he also filled the title role of the false messiah who in the end betrays his followers by embracing Islam. The sets were designed by Maxim, a renowned Rumanian painter, who brought the leading theatre personalities of Bucharest to see this highly stylized, surreal production that took the Vilna Troupe still further away from its earlier realistic style. The response was overwhelming.

Joseph Buloff in J. Zulawski's Sabbatai
Zvi, *Bucharest, 1924.*

While acknowledging a debt to Cocteau, Meyerhold, Chagall and Vakhtangov,
Buloff often insisted that the Theatre of the Absurd was endemic to Yiddish drama.
Years later, he wrote the following anecdote to prove this theory:

Recently, my friend Jack Garfein successfully presented two short plays by
Samuel Beckett at the Clurman Theatre on West 42nd Street. Typically, in one
of them, one actor reads in a monotone the same mumble-jumble over and over
again to another actor, who listens silently. That's the whole play! By the sixth or
seventh of 21 repetitive readings (by my own count), the audience was stupefied.
Even so, they put up with it and at the end applauded. People had just witnessed
dramatic modernity—a Theatre of the Absurd.

Modernity, my foot! I pioneered Theatre of the Absurd back in the Twenties.
All across Eastern Europe, I directed and starred in *Singer of His Sorrow*, the story
of Yoshke Musicant, an untutored musician who wins a lottery but gives away his
winnings so that the girl he loves can wed another. A good old tearjerker, but I
directed it as a fantasy seen though the eyes of a child—everything distorted, color-
enhanced and twice as large as life.

A few years after that production, while performing in another play in Paris I
received a telephone call from a young Rumanian who had just arrived in the West.
He hailed me as his idol and told me that he had seen *Singer of His Sorrow* in
Bucharest, where it had given him the clue to the type of anti-naturalist drama that
he was writing. I thanked him, wished him luck and forgot about him. But I
recognized his name when he became famous as the author of *The Bald Soprano*,
Rhinoceros and other similar masterpieces of the Theatre of the Absurd: Eugene
Ionesco.

The Theatre of the Absurd, however, antedates Ionesco, Beckett, Pinter and Durrenmatt, and even *The Singer of His Sorrow*, Buloff and the Vilna Troupe. It goes back one hundred years, to the early days of primitive Yiddish Theatre. By its very nature, the infant Jewish theatre had to be absurd because it grew out of the absurd situation of the Jews in Czarist Russia.

Imagine people who are more literate than any of their peasant neighbors—through the study of Talmud and Torah—but who are consigned to an inferior status and condemned to grinding poverty under arbitrary decrees barring them from land ownership and farming and confining them to a few ill-paying trades like tailoring, shoemaking and carpentry. The Jews were even forbidden under a harsh law to speak or use on the stage their own language, Yiddish.

Yet there was a hunger for culture in Jewish youths that impelled them to form Yiddish Theatre groups in spite of the law. They performed clandestinely in cellars or in barns and woodsheds at the outskirts of towns. When the secret police got wind of these theatrical activities, agents were sent with orders to halt the program if a single Yiddish word were uttered on the stage, and then to disperse the audience and arrest the cast. The Jewish players reacted by posting lookouts who would recognize any spies entering the makeshift theatre and would send a signal to the stage.

At that point, the actors would abruptly interrupt the Yiddish performance, and a thespian from Poland would embark on a recitation in Polish while a Hungarian would retort in Magyar. Those actors who knew only Yiddish would carry on a dialogue in meaningless gibberish: "Nov shmoz Kapap . . . " or something to that effect. The audience—in on the ruse—would sit impassively through the babble. And the spies would listen in puzzled incomprehension. What is this? Certainly not Russian, but not the forbidden Yiddish tongue, either. Then it would dawn upon them: "Aha, they are speaking French."

Whereupon the agents would take a drink and a bribe from the management, and depart with nothing to report. And presently the play would resume in Yiddish.

There you have it: a dozen actors on a bare stage, each one speaking a different language. Alienation, failure of communication, absence of objective meaning—all the elements of the Theatre of the Absurd! And it was invented from sheer necessity by Jewish actors a century ago.

Let me give Franz Kafka, himself a master of the absurd, the last word on the subject. After attending a Yiddish play in Prague, he wrote in his journal:

Joseph Buloff in O. Dimov's Singer of His Sorrow, *Rumania, 1925.*

"I will tell you, ladies and gentlemen, how much better you understand Yiddish than you imagine."

Buloff wrote about the success of *The Singer of His Sorrow* and *Sabbatai Zvi* in a mixture of elation and disenchantment in the following letter to his friend

Joseph Buloff in O. Dimov's Singer of
His Sorrow, *Rumania, 1925.*

and fellow actor Avrom Morevsky, who had left the
Troupe for an engagement in Berlin.

Bucharest
1925

Dear Rabbi (or, My dear old friend Morevsky):
I hesitate to put in writing my dreams and
despairs. But it would be a graver mistake to fail to
reply to your letter. So let me show you a handful of
ashes, and therein you might find a living ember of our
former holy flame.

Behold the tattered trophies of my endeav-
ors! Stand in awe before the blaze of my success! Listen
to the praises of my 40,000 admirers, half of whom are
not even Jewish! In fact, they make up the upper crust
of Rumania.

But to temper our enthusiasm, let us recall the
words of our fellow actor Baratov. At a gala performance, an admirer handed the actors a box of candies.
Baratov looked at it and exclaimed, "Oh candies,
candies, how you entrapped me into a life in the
theatre."

Don't get the impression that I am deaf to the
applause that by now has reached beyond the borders
of Rumania. I do frown, however, and remain more
or less unhappy. Today we play before kings and
ministers, but in the Yiddish Theatre, who knows
about tomorrow?

Can one know the value of vodka to a drunk? So let
us drink our vodka of artistic ambition to the very bottom of
the glass! For, in our anguished strivings, we actors are all
drunks.

But I forget that I am writing to you. To you,
Morevsky, who has drunk more than one glass of the theatre's
heady vintage.

So I rave on, like Baalam's ass in the Bible story when
it found its voice.

Hearty regards to your wife, and the same to both of
you from Luba. I have no more to say. A rabbi knows all. My
rabbi, you know, you know, you know.

Buloff

The success of *The Singer of His Sorrow* did "reach beyond the
borders of Rumania," opening the door to further adventures for
Joseph and me.

Invitation to America

From time to time, in the 1920's, stars of the Jewish theatre in America made guest appearances in Rumania. They would take the leading roles in popular Jewish-American plays and fill out their casts with local actors. Thanks to the pioneering work of our troupe, the Rumanian public accepted them with interest and even enthusiasm.

Molly Picon, the darling of light Yiddish operetta, played in Rumania on such a *gastrol* basis, and Celia Adler of the famed theatrical family also toured there.

In their spare time, they went to see the Vilner and came away deeply impressed. And on their return to the United States, they spoke about the brilliant new actor, Joseph Buloff, who doubled as an innovative and inspirational director. Such accolades soon made their way to Maurice Schwartz, the director and founder of the Yiddish Art Theatre. American-Jewish art theatre was synonymous with Maurice Schwartz. In a large new playhouse on Second Avenue and 12th Street—specially built for his company—he presented plays by Yiddish writers of the stature of Sholom Asch, Leivick, and I.J. Singer, for the more literate element of the Jewish public, and American theatre critics took respectful notice of his productions.

Schwartz himself was an imposing actor, a fine director and a highly experienced producer. In the mid-1920's his leading man, Muni Weisenfreund, left the Yiddish Art Theatre for Hollywood, where his sensitive performances turned him into the Oscar-winning film star, Paul Muni.

While searching for a replacement for Muni, Schwartz recalled the glowing reports of Molly Picon and Celia Adler on Joseph Buloff of the Vilna Troupe in Rumania, and wrote to invite Joe and me to come to New York and perform with the Yiddish Art Theatre.

This started a long correspondence between Buloff and Schwartz. Joseph had a desire both to perform and to direct in New York, the new center of Yiddish Theatre. But he had misgivings about new beginnings, as attested by the following letter to Leib and Chanah Kadison in America:

Rumania

Dear Parents:

I am writing with a broken pen. That is, I am writing, but it seems useless. Perhaps a telegram would better serve the purpose. Let me put my cards on the table, and enough of my indecision.

As matters stand now, my spirits are doing battle within me, and I am in agony. Saints and sinners deal easily with temptation, one way or the other, but mad spirits sink in self-doubt. Woe to them!

First I resolve to write to you, then my pen halts, because I don't know whether to bore you again with my problems or simply to write what I feel. If we had ship tickets, we would be on our way. But as things are, I need a trusted friend, to tell him about the conflicting advice that I have been getting from my two tempters.

One says, "Golem, whither art thou going? For gold, will you sell your soul? Have you not enough to eat? And honors up to your ears? What else do you want?"

The other one says, "What about room for growth? Are you content with applause from European audiences? America is a land of riches, where the golden-apple tree grows."

"Knucklehead," growls back the first voice, "Will you get to eat the golden apple? Will you be able to digest it? It is here, where you now are, that you found yourself, and here is where you will have to develop your talent. That is more important than your Schwartz contact."

                                                                Buloff

I myself favored a move to America for a variety of reasons. For one thing, I longed to be reunited with my family in New York, even though that meant parting with my other family, the Vilna Troupe, which had been such a big part of my life. For another thing, the Yiddish stage in America presented an exciting challenge. But my strongest impetus came perhaps from the memory of that anti-Semitic riot in Baden, organized by the budding Nazi Party, which had revived earlier memories of suffering during World War I. This caused me to wish for a safe shore and refuge from unknown and yet unnamed disasters.

As Buloff overcame his own doubts, he exacted from Schwartz certain commitments, which Schwartz eventually met. Our trip to America was assured. This did not mean, however, immediate departure. There were many details to be worked out: affidavits and visas to be secured, tickets to be sent to us, and ultimately assurances of employment and character references to be filed. So, between 1925 and 1927 we continued to play with the Troupe in Bucharest, Transylvania and other Rumanian provinces.

In Transylvania, tragedy struck. Late one night, I was awakened in my hotel room by moaning and screaming from the next room. I rushed in and found Judith Laress mortally ill and in great pain. But the next morning she insisted that we proceed with the scheduled performance near the town of Arad. As she got through her part as the hen woman in *The Singer of His Sorrow*, she collapsed. We took her by train, on a stretcher, to the hospital in Arad. Laress died the next day from the consequences of a burst appendix: peritonitis.

The Troupe had her buried in Arad and ordered an appropriately dignified gravestone. At the funeral, after paying tribute to the fine actress that she was, our managing director Mazo added the thought, "At least our sister died among us, and has us standing together at her graveside to mourn her. Who knows how we will end and who will be left to remember us?" Strangely prophetic words!

Once he had made up his mind to move on to the American-Yiddish stage, Buloff was impatient waiting for passage and a final, firm "Come!" from Schwartz. Again he wrote to Leib and Chana Kadison:

Satamar, 1926

Dear Parents:

We are writing to you, but we don't know what to write. At present, we are in the Transylvanian town of Satamar, which we struggled to get to but which, now that we are here, seems hardly worth the effort. A remote, backward region. Jews with earlocks down to the ground, who speak only Hungarian. In every townlet we are threatened with excommunication.

We are looking forward to proceeding to some larger cities, but in the meantime, we are cut off from the world. We get no letters. Our mail goes to the Czernowitz post office, which is supposed to forward it to us here, but usually it arrives a day after we have left.

We await our mail with impatience, because any day now I expect to receive a letter from Maurice Schwartz with the final offer to come to America. It would have been nice if we had a fixed residence at which to receive the important letter. But as things stand at the moment, we are in the unfortunate position of not knowing what to do.

Our contract with the Transylvania producer expires only at the end of August. Of course, it was signed long before we knew from your telegrams of the opportunity to join Maurice Schwartz's company. Now, without official word as yet, we don't have the courage to break the contract. If we already had the official paper, the necessary visas and passage on an ocean liner, we would quit. But, without these, we don't know what to do.

I'm waiting to get to Dej, where I hope to find my mail. Then I will know what to do. Meanwhile, all is quiet. The rest of the company knows nothing about our plans, though they sense that something is about to happen and hold their breath while waiting to see . . . .

Here, in Transylvania, we are presenting *The Dybbuk*, whose first act does not particularly strike our audiences: too gloomy for them. But they do like the second act, especially the laughs, and toward the end the play finally gets to them, and they listen respectfully.

Buloff

1927

Dear Parents:

Yesterday I got a letter; today a telegram. The contract has been signed. I felt a pang in my heart. Yes, and then no. Conflict.

The productions of *The Singer of His Sorrow* and *Sabbatai Zvi* have raised me to the top. Now I hold the reins of power and Alexander Stein is in the opposition. But the opposition is weak.

It would be foolish of me to complain at this point. I don't imagine that I would occupy the same high position in Schwartz's company.

Schwartz needs good actors. What he doesn't know is that I am an actor with a style of my own. I have my own conception of theatre. Since I fought here to have it recognized, I must naturally bring it to America. But if my approach is not the right one for America, it might be a mistake to import it.

Here, by contrast, the entire field is mine. Here, I am recognized as the only man who can say something and prove it. Yet my damned unrest, and concerns about tomorrow, propel me to think of America.

America is the great world. On the other hand, the Vilna Troupe is planning to return to Warsaw with *The Singer* and *Sabbatai Zvi*. To me, the prospect of again playing in Warsaw is most attractive. Yet I don't wish to abandon the thought of America—perhaps under the influence of Luba.

Because she is strongly in favor of moving on to America. But then, why leave the house that through great effort has been built by us? Why venture into the unknown?

I don't know how I will adapt to the dialect. It is not merely a matter of "kim" versus "kum." The point is that here we were devoted to the ideal of literary Yiddish. We strove to purify the language, and that was one of the great contributions of the Vilna Troupe. So it won't be easy to play serious roles in the dialect of the light-operetta theatre.

Today came a telegram giving us the date of our expected arrival in New York. Shall we cheer or weep?

We are now on our way to Transylvania to perform for six weeks, whereupon we can leave—which will probably be on July 25.

Hearty regards, and a kiss for Paula. Be well! Here's to our reunion in America.

Buloff

On to New York

The road to America lay open. We had a contract, visas, tickets and a fixed departure date. Upon completion of the tour, we bid farewell to our old friends in the Troupe and started on the long voyage to the U.S.A.

Following is a letter that Joe wrote on board, to Mazo.

July 26, 1927

Dear Mazo,

Sixth day between sky and water. At night, dark heavens, dark seas. Great white tongues lick the ship. A storm over the ocean.

The storm seeks out the ship. People are alarmed, cough, groan, vomit. I am all atremble. The white corridors of the ship become a hospital. Through the walls, I hear sighs, moans. And the sea roars.

An orchestra on the promenade deck plays loud music, as if to shut out the cry of the sea. Below, at the cinema, they are showing a film about an even greater storm, through which the liner Aquatania sailed. But few people watch it.

Today, the sea is quiet again. Somebody dies on board. He is awarded a sack and a stone, and is flung overboard into the sea.

The sun nobly rises. A well-dressed audience listens to the orchestra. What do I hear? A Goldfaden tune? America, Yiddish Theatre, here we come!

I meet a cantor. In America he is referred to as Rabbi. He is returning from a visit to his little home town and gets special kosher meals on the ship. He introduces himself to me as a noted cantor. "And you?"

"An actor."

"Good. Can you give me a free theatre ticket? Because New York is big, and I won't be able to find you there. Do you sing?"

"No. I am a dramatic actor."

"In America, you need to have a singing voice. Even to sell newspapers you must know how to sing."

I meet another Jew, from Chicago, and ask, "Have you seen the Vilna Troupe in America?"

"Yes."

"How did you like it?"

"They can't act."

"You don't say! What did you see them in?"

"Damned if I know. You can't make out a word they are saying."
The ship started to rock, so I ended the conversation.

Buloff

On arrival in New York, we were spared the ordeal of Ellis Island, for we were not entering as immigrants but as guest artists on temporary work permits. Nevertheless, a bureaucratic difficulty presented itself.

We were told that we had to post a $50 bond upon landing. A reasonable sum, except that we did not have it. Was it possible that, after our long journey, America would turn us away for lack of $50?

At the pier, Schwartz, accompanied by drama critic Hyman Ehrenreich of the Jewish daily, *The Forward*, had been waiting for his new actors. He saw hundreds of travelers coming down the gangplank, but nobody remotely resembling Buloff and Kadison. Had they missed the boat? Finally, Schwartz sent Ehrenreich aboard ship to investigate.

Ehrenreich found us sitting distraught in the purser's office and quickly solved our problem by posting $50 out of his own pocket. Then he escorted us off the ship and introduced us to Mr. Schwartz.

Although cordial enough, the great producer's eyes seemed to betray some doubt, as if he were saying to himself, "Are these the European stars I have promised my public—a couple of starving youngsters without $50 between them?"

Schwartz called a press conference the next day, at which Buloff was introduced as a veteran of the Russian Civil War in both the Red and the White Armies. Whereupon an irate left-wing reporter demanded to know how he could have served both sides.

Calmly, Joe explained that it had been simply a matter of survival; that each time he had been captured as a soldier in one army, he had been forced to switch to the other side to save his life. But his interrogator remained adamant: Didn't Mr. Buloff realize that a great ideal was at stake? Didn't he know that every soldier in the Red Army fought with a rifle in one hand and a copy of Karl Marx in the other?

"Nonsense," Buloff replied. "How do you suppose that as a seventeen-year-old Jew I managed to survive in the Red and White Armies? Only because the common soldiers on both sides were illiterate and needed me to write letters for them, did they share their rations with me and let me live. They would stand in sheer stupefaction by my side as I committed to paper their few broken words, and would mutter, '*Bozha moy!* Look, he can write!' So don't talk to me about soldiers marching with Karl Marx in their hands."

That started Buloff off on the wrong foot with the leftists in New York. But they nevertheless invited him a few days later to give, free of charge, a benefit performance for their newspaper—*The Freiheit*. Buloff was totally unaware of the paper's political complexion. Believing that he had been asked to help the cause of Yiddish, he accepted the invitation and gave the recital. The next morning an agitated Schwartz called Buloff and told him that Abraham Cahan, editor of the fiercely anti-Communist *Forward* had read about Buloff's appearance at The *Freiheit* affair and was furious. "You had better see him right away," Schwartz insisted.

Filled with trepidation, Joe made his way to The *Forward* office on East Broadway. After being excoriated by Cahan, for "lending aid and comfort to Soviet sympathizers," Buloff truthfully pleaded ignorance, as a newcomer, of the ideological shadings of the local press. He had simply been deceived. He spoke to the important Yiddish editor in Russian, because he had been tipped off that Cahan preferred speaking Russian to the Yiddish of his own newspaper.

Mollified either by Joe's fluent Russian or by what he had already heard about his contretemps with the Red American armchair general at the recent press conference, Cahan resolved to forgo a public denouncement in *The Forward*. But he would not grant Joe complete absolution for his naive error and decreed that for the time being the name Buloff was not to be mentioned in *The Forward*. As a result, for several months Buloff was referred to in theatre reviews as "the new talent from Europe."

We had been in America for less than ten days and already Buloff had gotten into hot water with both the Left and the Right. New York was going to be interesting.

We had a joyful reunion with my sister Paula and my parents. Leib and Chanah had been performing in small halls on the East Side with the Azro-Alomis company. It had been hard going, for the New York public was not ready for their low-key realistic style of acting or for their refined Litvak accent. For us, this constituted an early warning that we would have to modify our acting style and even our speech if we wished to succeed in this new land.

My parents had rented a room for us at Sea Gate, a Jewish resort community east of Coney Island. We spent our first summer there and traveled into Manhattan for rehearsals at the Yiddish Art Theatre.

Buloff played the youthful lead in *The Tenth Commandment* by Avrom Goldfaden, for which Schwartz had specifically engaged him. An elaborate spectacle, it fortunately did not prove to be overly successful, although Joseph's debut was well received.

The following letter to an unnamed friend contains Buloff's early impressions of America:

New York
Nov. 6, 1927

I don't know what to write first. Seventy things, each of sixty different colors. A variegated display of lights. Every day new impressions in a new reality. What looked gray to me yesterday turns red today. That which was sweet before is now tasteless. All I can do is observe, and I have become a light-prism that gathers all but retains nothing.

When I am interviewed by newsmen and introduce myself as Buloff of the Vilna Troupe, they frown. So I suppose this is not a big honor here.

The second Vilna Troupe is in America now performing at the Bowery—in the worst of theatres on the poorest street of drunkards. It breaks my heart to hear the gasps of my Vilna brothers' and sisters' dying souls! Alexander Azro has destroyed the second Vilna Troupe. For how long can he feed his people? They are trying to do melodrama, but they can't measure up even to Gebel's★ vest buttons. So they struggle.

Sonia Alomis' voice still rings with the same beauty it had some seventeen years ago. Leah Naomi is an able character actress. But Paula Walter is best appreciated here. Moishe Feder is not bad in some roles. Noah Nachbush continues to sing in his own special style. Azro is a talented actor, but here this does not count. There are countless good actors in America. Of course, good here means competent; that is, something less than what we used to call good in the old country. About

---

★ Gebel, with his wife Jennie Goldstein, was the leading producer of Yiddish melodrama.

Maurice Schwartz: Yiddish art theatre in America begins and ends with him. Visualize a pair of piercing Jewish eyes, a Hebraic nose and a folksy acting style. Offstage, a dusty hat and wrinkled coat, drooping socks and a badly knotted tie. When he is onstage, we see an impressive man with a genuine Jewish groan. Without a doubt, he would be great if only he stuck to suitable parts.

As an entrepreneur, he is the most important figure in Yiddish Theatre. Lots of energy, creative ability. But influential as he is as a producer, he is no less capable as a director. He has intuition and authority. He is opening his new theatre with *The Tenth Commandment* by Goldfaden—a very elaborate production.

As I watched a rehearsal of *The Tenth Commandment*, I recalled standing once with my stage manager at a performance in Rumania, shivering in the cold. Before walking on stage in the leading role, my dresser handed me one shoe. The other was missing.

Schwartz's production, by contrast, has everything. Achron— one of the most significant Jewish composers—is doing the music; Fokine—the great Russian ballet master—is the choreographer. And the stage settings are executed by the renowned Boris Aaronson. Lazar Weiner—one of the most talented young musicians—conducts the orchestra. High-fashion tailors are making the costumes. Director Schwartz is surrounded by close friends, advisers and plain loiterers who hang on his every word.

I take my hat off to Schwartz, because he rises at dawn, rushes right to the theatre and goes straight to bed as soon as the performance is over. His actors are the best on the Yiddish stage and all center around Schwartz.

My impression of the actor Jacob Ben-Ami: a charming shyness; black disheveled hair, soft-spoken on and Off Stage.

In *The Tenth Commandment* I have a small part, a bloodless one. But I have managed to squeeze something out of it.

The Yiddish Theatre in America: a solid iron spiderweb. The enmeshing strands are immigration quotas, troubles and anxieties of all sorts, Schwartz's theatre, the Hebrew Actors Union and Abe Cahan— creator of *The Forward* and czar of the Yiddish press.

For me it is a staircase, which I must carefully climb, watching my every step. But those who understand have already recognized me. They know what I can do.

Buloff

Schwartz's Yiddish Art Theatre

I did not have a part in *The Tenth Commandment*, but I was not left idle, for I played in the Yiddish Art Theatre's benefit repertory.

The benefit performance is one of the Yiddish Theatre's lasting contributions to the American stage. As a fund-raising device, an organization buys a block of tickets or even an entire performance, then sells the tickets at a mark-up to its members and supporters. So everyone benefits. The organization makes a profit for its charitable purposes. Its members enjoy an evening in the theatre and a tax deduction for the part of the ticket price that is considered a charitable contribution. And the producer is guaranteed a sold-out house. Also, benefit performances generate work for actors.

Joseph Buloff (right) and O. Dimov presenting The Singer of His Sorrow *to Maurice Schwartz, New York, 1927.*

S. Asch's Witch of Castille, *New York, 1928. Left to right (in cage): Stella Adler, Maurice Schwartz, Joseph Buloff.*

Schwartz played the benefit game to the hilt. In addition to his featured productions, he had a repertoire of tried-and-true plays like *Tevye and God of Vengeance.* At a moment's notice, he would pull these out for a benefit performance and present newcomers like me with the tremendous challenge of having to memorize the parts overnight, rehearse them in the morning under the direction of the stage manager and deliver a polished performance that same evening. The experience was great, but the work hard.

After *The Tenth Commandment,* Buloff was given a chance to stage, direct and star in *The Singer of His Sorrow.* Celia Adler wanted to play the girl Rosalie, but Joe insisted that I keep my old part.

Schwartz portrayed Simoncheck, the seducer; Anna Appel, his mother; and Bertha Gersten, Sheineh. Despite the strong cast and its European reputation, however, the play did not become a hit at its first New York presentation. The cast lacked unity with its diverse dramatic styles and manners of speech. Besides, the poetic quality of the production was rather strange to the Second Avenue audience of that time.

We rented a one-room flat on Second Avenue, within walking distance of the theatre. We studied English, and we prepared for our second season with Maurice Schwartz.

It opened with *The Witch of Castille* by Sholem Asch. Stella Adler had the title role, and Schwartz played her father, the patriarch, while Joe portrayed the Pope and I, a Spanish courtesan.

In the climactic scene, Stella, accused of witchcraft, is imprisoned in a cage with her old father. Buloff, as the Pope, comes to plead with them to embrace the Cross and save their lives. In this extremely difficult scene, he won an unexpected ovation from the Jewish public by the warmth and humanity of this portrayal and by a parting gesture of blessing that seemed to embrace the entire audience.

In those days, the celebrated critic Harold Clurman was courting Stella Adler and often attended her performances. Impressed by Buloff's performance as the Pope, Clurman wrote in an article in the Theatre Guild's publication that he was a star of the first magnitude.

Next came *Uncle Moses* by Asch. Schwartz had the leading role, and Buloff, though much younger, played his father—a simple, pious Jew. Stella Adler played the leading female part. The next production of the season was a Russian play, *Man with Portfolio*; and we also appeared in numerous benefits.

The Hebrew Actors Union, a major force, controlled the Yiddish stage in America in such vital matters as membership eligibility, wages and conditions of employment. Its example impelled American performers to organize their own union, the Actors Equity. Thus, the unionization of the entertainment industry became another contribution of the Jewish stage to the American theatre.

Joe and I were obliged to apply for membership in the Hebrew Actors Union, which entailed auditioning before as many members as cared to attend. First I did a scene as Leah in *The Dybbuk*, then a monologue from *The Novala*. Joe auditioned after me. We were accepted on the first try.

Joseph Buloff in A. Faiko's Man With Portfolio, *New York, 1928.*

In two seasons, we had established ourselves as valued members of the best Yiddish Theatre company. We should have been content, but we were not.

We had been accustomed to playing as an ensemble within a permanent company, a style of life and acting for which the Vilna Troupe was renowned. By contrast, Schwartz, although he had some regular actors, followed a system of hiring players as the need arose each season. The Yiddish of his stage was not the elegant literate language that the Vilner used. The Vilna Troupe would rehearse each play for months on end before its premiere. With Schwartz, we often had to prepare a role within a day.

Joseph found little room for his directorial ambitions. While his respect for Schwartz as producer, director and actor was considerable, he felt the strain of a natural rivalry between two leading men.

As for Schwartz, I think he was a little afraid of Buloff. He seldom addressed him directly, using me to convey messages. With me, he was invariably polite and even chivalrous.

The newcomer's sense of wonderment and confusion in confronting the American scene were expressed by Buloff in his letter to Morevsky:

New York

Dear Morevsky,

I received your letter full of the usual insults.

True, I overate on success in Rumania and got a swollen belly. So I went to America for a cure. And it has worked.

I appreciate the words of my old rabbi, but please know, America is not paradise, but it's not a garbage dump either. On Second Avenue—the Jewish street—there is a concentration of Yiddish Theatres, and there are twenty-five more all over the country. There also is a union of Yiddish actors with a membership of 450.

A city of bustling streets, iron buildings and paper Dollars. Bitter antagonism between leftists and rightists in the Yiddish press.

I have not closed the door on Europe. It is rather that—despite the quota laws—a window has opened for me to America. I look through the window and I think: Europe, with her meager breasts filled with the poisoned milk of anti-Semitism, bespattered your todays and plunged you into a dark depression about your tomorrows.

From all quarters of the world, America draws prominent artists, and here they dissolve under the power of the Dollar. The Dollar is the underhanded, sadistic extinguisher of our artistic flame.

If, as it is said, France teaches the world, England thinks for the world, and Russia suffers for the world, then America tells the world, "Kiss my . . ." And everyone does, because anyone who refuses is a greenhorn.

And to be green here is worse than to be red. Because red here has a different shade. A red in this land takes a nice bath in the morning, finds a bottle of fresh milk delivered at his doorstep, and then climbs into his own automobile to drive to a Sunday meeting of 10,000 radicals, where the police keep order and protect the speakers. That takes away the meaning and flavor of the word red.

Why am I going on in this reportorial vein? Just to keep the conversation going.

Buloff

P.S. You may be disappointed this letter contains nothing personally pleasing to you. I will only add, without admitting that you are the only European actor who is favorably mentioned here, that every living being should see America. And, if you get a chance, I would advise you without a doubt: Run, don't walk!

I hope that at least this P.S. will elicit an answer from you. I have given you the start of the ABC's on America, so send back some cheerful news from Riga.

Greetings to all actors who know me; greetings from all actors who know you. Luba sends hearty regards, and best wishes to your wife from both of us. The Kadisons add their greeting: old regards from the old Vilna Troupe.

Chicago

In 1928 Joseph Buloff left Maurice Schwartz's company and became director of the Yiddish Dramatishe Gesellschaft—an amateur troup in Chicago, Illinois. To the Jewish theatre world, this would have been tantamount to Sir Laurence Olivier's desertion of the London stage to manage a provincial repertory theatre in Liverpool. The Jewish press and public could not understand why a star of established European reputation who had also made his mark on the New York

Joseph Buloff in J. Zulawski's Sabbatai Zvi, *Chicago, 1928.*

stage would even consider associating himself with a non-professional company in the Midwest.

Yet Buloff had valid reasons for doing it. His ambition to direct experimental plays of his own choosing had been largely frustrated by the indifference of both the Yiddish Art Theatre's management and the New York press. With the example of the original Vilna Troupe before him, he believed that art theatre could best be served by a group of dedicated, talented amateurs, fired by enthusiasm for high literary drama.

Therefore, when the managing directors of the Yiddish Dramatishe Gesellschaft contacted him from Chicago with a proposal, he carefully weighed his options. The Gesellschaft was connected to the Jewish People's Institute of Chicago, which had just built a fine new theatre. News of Buloff's ground-breaking work as a a director and actor in Europe and New York had reached them, and they offered him the position of leading man and director for the coming season. Included in the offer was the position of leading lady for me.

When Buloff brought the proposal to me, I readily agreed to the change. Like him, I felt uncomfortable with the audiences of the commercial Yiddish stage in New York. Chicago offered us an opportunity to revive our own repertory—an interesting challenge. We accepted the Gesellschaft's offer.

Our first play in Chicago was *Sabbatai Zvi*, in which Buloff played the title role and I was his temptress. Free to use his imagination as adapter and director, Buloff costumed me exactly like himself as Sabbatai Zvi. So, through me, he symbolized the false messiah's alter ego. The stylized production was enthusiastically acclaimed by the Chicago critics.

Later that season we did *The Singer of His Sorrow*, *A Play Without a Name* and Leivick's *Shop*. In all of them Buloff and I played the leading roles, with a supporting cast from the Gesellschaft: working people, mostly young, who came to rehearsals at the Jewish People's Institute every evening after their regular jobs. The group performed only on weekends. Without pay, solely for the love of theatre, the actors put in long hours of rehearsal, learned their lines, painted scenery, stitched costumes. Here Buloff discovered Abe Feder, today one of the leading lighting designers in the profession. Another find was the set designer Ziporin, who went on to become a prominent American artist. Mason was our company manager and a reliable supporting actor.

The Gesellschaft was subsidized by the Chicago Jewish community, but our most substantial single backer was Jacob Dubov, a wealthy sporting-goods manufacturer and devoted Yiddishist. Apart from being our company's Maecenas, Dubov and his wife, Sarah, became good friends of ours.

There were triumphs and there were disappointments in Chicago, and Buloff recounted them in letters to friends and fellow actors.

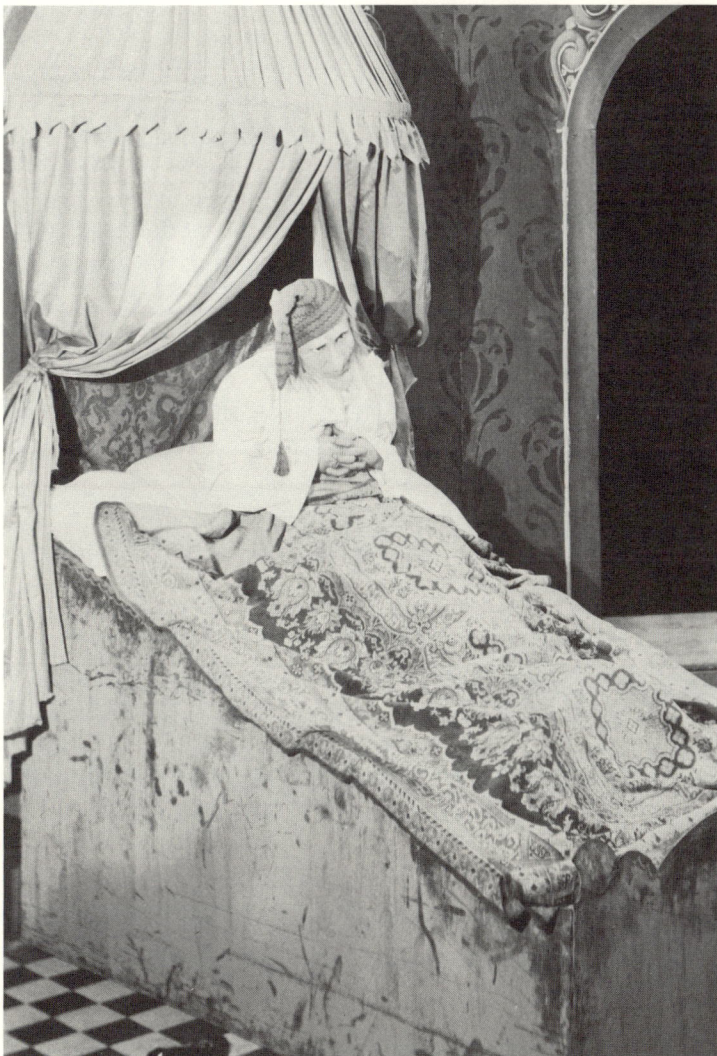

Joseph Buloff in Molière's The Miser, *Chicago, 1929.*

To Moishe Nadir, Yiddish writer and humorist:

Chicago
1928

Dear friend Nadir,

Your Sholom Aleichem requires more than a simple Aleichem Sholom.

I am working in Chicago now with a group of young people whose ambition is to create something artistic. Our first presentation was *Sabbatai Zvi* by Zulawski; the second, *The Singer of His Sorrow* by Osip Dimov; the third, *A Play Without a Name*. All three plays made a spectacular splash, as if a heavy rock had been thrown into the shallow pond of the Chicago theatre. People have begun to show an interest in us. Remarkably, most of those who noticed our work are not even closely associated with the Jewish community or even with Jewish culture.

None of our twenty-five members get paid. The physical conditions are good, with a substantial playhouse owned by an organization called the Jewish People's Institute. It has little interest in Yiddish language and culture. Though it tolerates us, it wants to squeeze the last cent out of us and charges quite a fee for the theatre. Furthermore, the theatre is closed on Fridays, the best night, and on Saturdays, too. This casts a dark shadow on our enterprise.

For each offering, we build and paint new scenery and make our own costumes. Let me tell you that for each play we hold no less than sixty rehearsals, which means that the box office cannot carry the expenses, and there has to be a substantial subsidy.

I and Luba Kadison and a couple of employees are the only ones on salary. Minimal but something. The committee of the Institute deserves a big thank you for its interest, even though the interest is only casual. We exist, good! If we didn't, they wouldn't sit *shiva* for us. So our best endeavors cannot bring us healthy existence.

All this we could endure were it not for the biggest problem: a boycott by *The Forward* newspaper. The Hebrew Actors Union has blacklisted us because our actors are non-professionals and not eligible for membership. In plain language it has forbidden *The Forward* to write about us, while *The Freiheit* paper is denying us publicity from the Left. And so, my friend, we are left shooting blanks in the air.

Stubborn though I am, this presses on my heart like a lead weight. I can stand it, but I must admit it bothers me.

Our company has a certain amount of talent and a great measure of devotion. Without any question, we have the potential to produce good work.

Announcement of The Singer of His Sorrow, *Chicago, 1927.*

Most of our members have wives, children. They work at their regular jobs during the day and come to rehearsals every night. For that effort alone, they deserve all the credit. They also help out financially.

Although the work is hard and our pay small, their enthusiasm gives me satisfaction. There are compensations, but I can't see any future in it.

That is why your letter about a Workers Theatre stirred my actor's imagination. Not only am I interested, I am intrigued. But how do you get the bear over the mountain?

You say that your proposal is unofficial as yet. Therefore my reply must be unofficial as well. So it remains up in the air, and this is just a casual letter: an Aleichem Sholom to your Sholom Aleichem.

Yours,
Buloff

P.S. Write and I will reply promptly. I have been busy preparing Leivik's *Shop*. That was the only reason for my delay in answering.

Chicago, 1928

Dear Morevsky,

Though far apart, we remain friends. Your letter gave me great joy. Knowing me, you realize that wherever fate takes me, I leave a piece of my heart. And when I receive a reminder of my past in a letter, I appreciate it as does a child who has received an unexpected gift.

Things with you, I see, are still the same. The Messiah has not come yet.

Here, we cannot complain. Our Jews multiply, and in New York their numbers have almost reached the total promised by the Almighty to Father Abraham. The Jews love theatre, even if it is naive and childish. That is why Jewish actors have cars and money in the bank.

I am considered a simpleton despite my status as a star. It is my fate to remain a pauper forever and ever. The simple reason is that I am a Talmudic scholar of sorts who believes that the theatre must be served with the same devotion as the Torah. You have to beg for your bread and pray with all your might that in the next world the Master of the Universe will serve you a portion of leviathan from His own hand.

True, American fish are better than leviathan. But you need money to buy them. For a long time, I was uncertain whether to buy American fish or wait patiently for leviathan. Finally, I decided for the leviathan. I left the great temple in New York, with its thousand false lights, and settled in a humble synagogue lit by a single, true candle, where I serve the Holy Order of the Theatre. That, in short, is the rabbinical explanation of my American experience.

Buloff

Joseph Buloff in Molière's The Miser, *Chicago, 1929.*

To Itzhak Kadison:

Dear Itzhak,

Thank you for sending me Pinchik's* book. It gave me great pleasure. The past is veiled in nostalgia, and regardless of what lies under the veil, one always has the urge to lift it again. Pinchefsky, Rumania, Bucharest—I recall it all.

Once Pinchefsky invited me to his lodgings to read me his poems. He lived in a hotel that bore the symbolic name, "Egypt." In Yiddish, "Mitzraim." If Mitzraim looked like that hotel, I can understand why the Jews remember it in pain unto this day.

On entering the hotel, I faced a problem. A dead cat lay across the corridor. I could easily jump over it, but then I would have had to land in a pile of . . . . I managed to get past these obstacles to reach a rickety staircase. Here I had to watch my step because one wrong move and I would not have climbed up but fallen down into the cellar.

By care and skill, I reached the first floor, when suddenly I heard a raucous cry: "Get away! A curse on your father! Get out of here or I will split your head!" I felt like taking to my heels and fleeing. But then I heard a familiar voice replying softly: "I will pay you when I can—take my hands, take my ears, but give me back my notebook. I have to read my poems to Buloff."

Another time, I remember, Pinchefsky was an extra in one of our plays, and he disguised himself by painting a third eye on his forehead. All the actors were impressed by his originality. Unfortunately, when he got on stage he lost his nerve and stood with his back to the audience.

Going off, he asked, "What do you say, Buloff? Did I make a hit with my front or with my back?"

All this aside, his discussions with fellow writers are among the best of my memories of Bucharest. His witty criticism always hit the nail on the head. My best regards to him.

Of our present work, I could write more, but I don't know if it would interest you, because the issues of theatre art and our circumstances in Chicago are so alien to and distant from Russia that they can hardly be explained.

In general, I am reluctant to talk about what is still only an experiment here. This much is clear, however: we have caused an uproar here, cut ourselves off from the entire theatre world and made a million enemies plus three million more who regard me as a madman. But the pot of soup is still boiling. Are we going to have to eat it by ourselves? We shall see.

Again I ask you, dearest Itzhak, please send me some Yiddish or Russian plays (postage guaranteed). Send me also material about *Cement* by Glatkov. It is the only Russian play that made an impression here. I am sure I won't have to ask you a third time. A thousand thanks in advance.

Buloff

* Pinchefsky, a Yiddish writer in Bucharest, Rumania.

To Botoshansky (Jewish journalist and playwright in Buenos Aires):

Chicago, 1928

A year ago, I parted company with the professional Yiddish Theatre and came to Chicago, where we are trying to lay a foundation and carry the bricks for the building of a new theatre. I found a group of young people whose help and enthusiasm keeps me going. Under the name of Chicago Dramatishe Gesellschaft, they have hitched themselves to the rickety wagon of Yiddish art theatre and at great sacrifice are pulling it uphill.

You know how a theatre is built. It takes either a German occupation or a Russian revolution. Since naturally such things do not occur here, we turned to the good old custom of going from door to door with a collection plate.

Chicago has a Jewish community of 400,000; it is easier to collect contributions here than in most other places.

Sabbatai Zvi was our first production. As you know, I had done it earilier with the Vilner in Bucharest. Returning to the same story, I now rekneaded it and baked it fresh. As a result, the play scored 100 percent—fifty percent old, fifty percent new.

For my second presentation, I similarly led my *Singer of His Sorrow* to the baths, washed him, cleansed him, shaved him, and attired him in new garments. And he sang his old songs in a new way.

The third selection was brand-new: *A Play Without a Name*. It is an old piece that could have had a name, yet the non-title enabled a critic to comment sharply that "It is an interesting experiment to offer the American public A Play Without a Name, when it is accustomed to a name without a play." Ninety-three rehearsals of three hours each were necessary to get the staging right.

Next came *Shop*. Fifty percent of the credit for its success should probably go to the author, Leivick, who after each performance delivered wonderful thank-you speeches. The remaining fifty percent, however, is due to the direction and acting. With that we ended our season.

We gave about fifty performances. This was truly one of the finest things that I have done in my stage career. I received your books. As busy as I am, the

Joseph Buloff as Wolf in H. Leivick's Shop, *Chicago, 1928.*

name Herschele Ostropoler so excited me that I dropped everything and read your play. I have no definite opinion as yet. At the moment, I am working on an interesting spectacle, which totally absorbs me, but as soon as I am finished with it, I think I will try the Herschele piece, because I am stirred by the man's folksy influence on the Yiddish stage. For reminding me of him, you deserve thanks.

לייוויק וואך

אראנזשירט פון דעם

שלום עליכם פאלק־אינסטיטוט
שיקאגא

אנטאנגענדיג

שבת, דעם 10טן מערץ, 1928

אין אירישען פאלקס אינסטיטוט

3500 דאגלאס בולוואר

פרילינג באל

מאכם זיך גריים פאר דעם פרילינג באל גענעבן פון די שלום
עליכם פרויען קלוב. פאר ווייטערדיקע אינפארמאציע פאלגם
נאך אונדזער אנאנס.

ה. לייוויק אפשיד אוונט
מיטוואך דעם 28־מן מארטש
אין פיפלס אינסטיטוט מעאטער

גרויסע איבעראשונג. — צום ערשטן מאל וועם ה. לייוויק
אליין אויפטרעטן צוזאמען מים דער דראמאטישער געזעלשאפט
אין זיין „גולם"

פון פערטע סצענע מאסן דעקלאמאציע

פאסיקע רייכע פראגראם מים באוואוסטע ארטיסטן צוזאמען
מים יוסף בולאוו און ליובא קאדיסאן

איינצלהיים פון דער פראגראם וועם קירצלאך אנאנסירם ווערן.
גריים זיך שוין צו מים גוטע פלעצער צו באקומען
אין קאסע פון מעאטער.

שיקם אייערע קינדער אין דער שלום עליכם שול
פון אייער גענומ:

שול איינס, 3238 וו. דיווזישאן גאס
שול צוויי, 2734 וו. דיווזישאן גאס
שול פיר, 3657 וו. פאלק גאס
שול פינף, 3659 נ. מענטראל פארק עוו.

אין אונדזערע שולן ווערן געלערנט די פאלגענדע לימודים

1) אידישע שפראך, לייענען, שרייבן, גראמאטיק און
קאמפאזיציע
2) די אידישע ליטעראטור, קלאסישע און מאדערנע
3) אידישע געשיכטע, אלטע און נייע
4) געזאנג, ארבעטער און פאלקס לידער
5) מאלעריי
6) קלארקיים אין אידיש־זשעלטשאבע אין ארבעטער
ענינים

אחוץ דעם קריגם דאס קינד א דערציאונג אין ברייטסטן
מענשלעכן באגריף

פאר מער אינפארמאציע ווענדם זיך צום שלום עליכם
פאלק אינסטיטום, 2734 וועסט דיווזישאן גאס, טעלעפאן
ארמיפיידזש 1462

Jewish Art Players

Affiliated with the

PEOPLES INSTITUTE

 "SHOP"

(Drama in 4 acts) by H. LEIVICK

Produced by JOSEPH BULOFF

CAST ACCORDING TO THEIR APPEARENCE

Old Leizer .... Ben Zion Gordon
Wolf, a boss .... Joseph Buloff
Gould, another boss .... Markus Meizel
Barkan, designr .... Morris Mason
Hymie, cutter .... J. W. Avedenko
Young Woman .... Ida Wolinsky
1st Operator .... Benjamin Fishbein
Ber, presser .... M. Isenberg
Minnie, operator .... Luba Kadison
3rd operator .... W. Verona
Shloime Haym, presser .... Samuel Rubenstein
Young Man .... S. Arnoff
Katie) operators .... Taubel Liessin
Sadie) .... F. Kaplan
Gertie, finisher .... Anna Swiet
Lipman, operator .... David Davidson
Phillip, cutter .... Sol Gendin
Benny, operator .... H. Shusterman
Leibl, cutter .... Oscar Hussman
Rayie .... Sarah Patt
1st slugger .... Joseph Casper
2nd Slugger .... Jonah Greenberg

Scenery produced at CARSON'S STUDIO
Scetches designed by MITCHEL SIPORIN

All shop equippment furnished by the courtesy of the firm
of JOSEPH SALTZMAN, 571 West Van Buren Street.
Our appreciation to Mr. J. Saltzman.   Jewish Art Players.

פאלקס אינסטיטוט טעאטער

(שיקאגער דראמאטישע געזעלשאפט)

 „שאפ"

(דראמע אין 4 אקטען) פון ה. לייוויק

אויפגעפירט פון יוסף בולאוו

פערזאנען לוים זייער דערשיינונגען אף דער בינע

דער אלטער לייזער (היטער פון שאפ) .... בן ציון גארדאן
וואלף, א באם .... יוסף בולאוו
גולד, צווייטער באם .... מאקל מייזל
בארקאן, א דעזיינער .... מארים מייסאן
היים, קאטער .... יעקב אוואדענקא
יונג ווייבעל .... איידא וואלענסקי
ערשטער אפערייטאר .... בנימן פישביין
בער, א פרעסער .... מאיר אייזנבערג
מינע, אפערייטארין .... ליובא קאדיסאן
דריטער אפערייטאר .... וועלוול וואראנא
שלמה היים, א פרעסער .... שלמה רובענשטיין
יונגערמאן .... שמואל ארנאף
קיידי, אפערייטארין .... מיכל ליעסין
סיידי .... פיגל קאפלאן
גוידי, פינישערין .... אנא סוויעט
ליפמאן, אפערייטער .... דוד דייווידסאן
פיליפ, א קאטער .... שלמה גענדין
בעני אפערייטער .... צבי שוסטערמאן
לייבל, א קאטער .... אשר נחומאן
ראיע .... שרה פאט
ערשטער שמארקער .... יוסף קאספער
צווייטער שמארקער .... יונה גרינבערג

דעקאראציעם אויסגעפירם פון קארסאנם סטודיא לוים די סקי־
צען פון מיכל ציפארין.

Program of Chicago, 1928 production of Shop.

What is new in your theatre world? What do you hear from Morevsky? Schwartz spoke to me about him, and I believe that he will engage him for next season.

Now, what do you think of the idea that Luba and I should seek our fortunes on your Argentine soil? Since America is a land where everything is possible, it is also possible that I may be forced to leave it. Because I entered on a six-month work permit, and I have stayed for two years.

It might be ordained that we work together on Herschele Ostropoler in Argentina's new art theatre. What do you say? I await your letter.

Buloff

Temporary Parting

Since Joseph's letters treat mostly theatrical subjects, it falls upon me to describe our life in Chicago. Our combined earnings from the Gesellschaft were paltry, and we lived in one single room in a carpenter's apartment. Our gruff landlord disapproved of our unconventional actors' hours, denied us kitchen privileges and thus forced us to take our meals in a little restaurant—the Blue Kretchma, which offered inexpensive Jewish-style fare and served as a kind of hangout for our company.

In our spare time, we went on with our English lessons, and I resumed playing piano. I rented an upright, which obviously did not fit in our crammed quarters but which the landlord allowed me to place in his living room in exchange for teaching his seven-year-old daughter to play it. For myself, I engaged a teacher, who a few months later invited me to participate in a recital with her other pupils.

With some trepidation—only because I was older than the other pupils—I accepted, and confidently began with a Chopin piece. In the middle, however, I lost my way, hesitated and broke off—then cried bitterly backstage. How could I, who had faced hundreds of audiences without the slightest display of nervousness, collapse at a mere amateur musical recital? It had happened partly because I was assaying a strange medium, and partly—or mainly—because of deep-seated frustrations.

Summer had come early to the Midwest, and Chicago was sweltering in a heat wave. I was bored, with too much time on my hands. In Europe, surrounded by Vilna Troupe friends, I always had plenty of theatrical activities and social contacts to occupy me. In New York City, the learning of new roles had kept me overworked but absorbed. In Chicago, on the other hand, I performed only on weekends and played mostly parts with which I was overly familiar. While I well understood that Joe had to devote most of his time to the preparation of scripts and the tightening of the company, I often felt lonely. My best option seemed to be to make a trip to New York, to spend the summer with my sister Paula and my parents.

During the train ride, I committed to paper my thoughts and frustrations, and wrote to Joe about them.

New York City
June 29, 1929

My Dearest:

    Here I am in hectic, noisy New York! I will try to relay all my impressions from the moment I left you at the station in Chicago.

    The ride was like one long yawn. At every station we stopped for at least twenty minutes, sometimes for an hour. I read, dreamed, ate, napped, and still failed to fill the time.

I began to write, letting my pen run across the paper without purpose. I wanted to talk to someone—and ended up opening my heart to the piece of paper.

You might laugh at this. But I promised to write; I will now confess in writing what I never had the courage to say to you. My notes from the train:

The road is long and lonely, my destination distant.

Lofty is my ambition, but few are my creative achievements. Will I find the strength to give flesh and blood to my ambitions and make my dreams come true?

Now my road is misty, but through the fog I try to see a light. For without clarity, my life would lose its purpose.

But fog envelopes me all the same. I fear that I am a burden to myself and to you. And the mist grows thicker, the clouds darker.

Then suddenly through the fog I glimpse a bright road ahead. Again faith and enthusiasm arise in me, as I envision us going hand in hand, confidently striding on our chosen way toward our dream. A heavy weight falls off our shoulders.

Don't be afraid of the word *dream*! The only sure way to our dream is to help each other with kind words and gentle feelings. With kindness and love we can surmount the difficulties that stand in the way of our theatrical destinies. Because the theatre is sacred for both of us. Theatre to us is a healing potion and ambrosia for our thirsting spirits. Do not destroy my faith! Let me share with you in the building of the artistic theatre that you envision in your fervid imagination.

These are the words that the wheels sang to me on the long ride to New York City. When the train finally arrived at Penn Station, my heart was full of expectancy and anxiety.

Imagine my disappointment at finding no one to greet me at the terminal. I got into a cab, which took me to 170 Second Avenue, and there I saw a fine new apartment house with two doormen in gold-buttoned livery at the entrance. I found an astonished Henry (Paula's husband) who knew nothing about my telegram; it had never arrived. Shortly thereafter, Papa came in and there was a great celebration. We embraced and danced like little children.

Mama and Paula are in the Catskill Mountains. Monday I am going to join them.

New York is still New York. Same Second Avenue, same Cafe Royale, same faces. But the sign on Maurice Schwartz's Yiddish Art Theatre has changed, with top billing for Misha and Lucy Gehrman. I met various actors, including Mr. Gehrman. He asked me to write you about an engagement for us, and he wants you to write and respond to his offer.

Haven't had the honor of meeting Mr. Schwartz yet. All are cordial, and compliment me on my healthy appearance. Deep in their hearts, I think they envy our position in Chicago. All show great respect for you.

I saw *The Fall of Petersburg*, one of the most impressive films I have ever seen. In my next letter I will write you more about the theatre scene in New York.

Meanwhile, be well and take care of yourself! Eat well, enjoy yourself!

I kiss you. Regards from all our friends. Regards to all.

Your Luba

In reply, Buloff wrote the following letters to me from Chicago:

Chicago
July 3, 1928

Dear Luba,

I have always believed that like Eve, you were created from my rib. While reading your letter, I had the uncanny feeling that I was reading my own writing. Five or six years of living together is enough time for sensitive people to influence each other. With us, this mutual influence has been such that if I put one of your letters into my records and shortly thereafter reread it, I would take it for a copy of one of my own.

Like you, as soon as you left, I found myself wondering how to get through the day. Something was missing. With nobody to ask me where I was going, I did not know where to go. And with nobody to ask me, "What are you going to do?" I had nothing to do.

On my return from the Kretchma Restaurant, I streched out on the couch in my clothes, put on the scratchy phonograph, and tried to rest. Still, I pondered, dreamed a thousand dreams and by morning came to the firm conclusion that we will stay together for the next 120 years.

It is true that during the past few weeks I sensed your discontent. You said nothing, but that little nose of yours that gets long and pointed when you are unhappy drilled deep into me, and your silence was your reproach to me—that I don't concern myself enough with you, that life has become too narrow for you, that life here is unsatisfactory, that you miss the excitement of creation, that I have taken over all the artistic work. Naturally, you are too fine a lady to say it aloud. So you protest through silence.

If truth be known, you and I are moody people. When I am in a bad mood, I roam the streets, or leaf through dusty books, or meet with boring people and pretend to listen to their boring talk even as I think my own thoughts, or I go off to a quiet corner and wait until the bad mood passes. It is different with you. When you are unhappy, you communicate your mood to me, and if I do not respond, you take it to mean I am distant and not one with you.

The present situation in our theatre is not bad—thank God, I am doing some good work—even if there is still much anxiety and concern in me, topped of course by your brooding letter. But, you see, your trip to New York has brought quick relief to both of us, for on the very next morning, I made my resolution to extend my agreement with you for another 120 years.

I continue to work at the Jewish People's Institute. The work goes on, but our group is tired, and it is hard for me to get it together for rehearsals in this heat.

I attended a lively meeting of the Gesellschaft. Dubov is enthusiastic, but the organization still doesn't have the money.

I spent several days with the actor Itkin. Seems to be a good sort. He slept over a few nights and could have stayed longer were he not such a snorer. He shook the house.

Every morning after breakfast, I go straight to the Institute. I turn on the fans in the big room, open all four windows, and the place cools off. The streets of Chicago are dreadfully hot. I sit at my desk for four, five hours, and I work. I have three acts ready to play, and one more will surely be done. I could start rehearsals this week. But first I want to see if we can get organized and have some guarantee for next season. And I want to wait for this heat to subside: it seems to be getting worse, however.

On August 12, our U.S. residence permit expires, which means that is is time to start working on an extension. First of all, you have to go to the HIAS to speak to Ignatov. The rest, I will say in my next letter.

Your Buloff

Chicago
July 1928

Dear Luba,

My last letter brought you very little good news. That's our luck; just as you got away from all the confusion and anxieties, to catch your breath, I had to write about and burden you with the most recent problem.

The situation is the same. I still do not know in which world I am. As I wrote you, it is time to apply for an extension to stay in America. Therefore I called that pest Atlas and made an appointment to meet him.

That evening I was busy until 11 p.m., then took the trolley and reached his house after midnight. He had bought new furniture and a radio. The *schmendrick*! He and his madame treated me to a dried-out apple, and we spoke about the $1,000. First he took the $130—interest on the money he paid out. Now he says that $130 doesn't count. He took it, and that's that! And now he is withdrawing the $1,000 bond and will not deposit it again for our extension.

You can imagine how I felt. He is right, of course; the $1,000 should have been repaid to him by now. But what is to be done?

Let somebody else put up the bond, he says. He doesn't want to be bothered anymore. I began to speak, to plead with him, because I realize that as soon as he withdraws his $1,000, we will have to leave the country and return to Europe.

This time the Gesellschaft won't make the same effort they made last year to find another $1,000. Nor will our patron Dubov lift a finger to help.

In short, I pleaded with Atlas until tears came to my eyes. Not because I am afraid that we would have to leave the United States, but because I felt like spitting in his face. In the presence of his radio and new furniture, however, I hesitated to do it. So, instead of spitting through my mouth, I squeezed the liquid out through my eyes.

It was 3 a.m. when I left him—too late for the trolley—so I walked and walked for two and a half hours, until my rage cooled off.

Nothing is moving at the Gesellschaft, Dubov is still in New York, and without him there is nothing to talk about. On Friday we are giving a free performance. I will read something without pay. The idea is to get the public to come free of admission charge, and then to get them to buy subscriptions for next season. We'll see how it works.

I would not like to return to Europe this year. But my heart somehow tells me that this year we will say farewell to America. I wrote to Botoshansky, the drama critic, and hinted that we might try our luck with him in Argentina. I am waiting for his reply.

Be well! In the snapshot you sent me, you look like a true blue-blooded princess—slim and beautiful—a treat for the eye!

Be sure to build up on your strength in the meantime.

Your B.

Chicago
July 1928

Dear Luba,

First a compliment: you write splendid letters—short, sharp, simple, truly a pleasure to read. Nor am I, your loving husband, the only one of this opinion; all to whom you have written think so. They cannot express enough admiration.

The literary evening was a success. Over 700 people packed the house. Some walked out because it was too hot and because there wasn't enough room. Even those who say that large crowds showed up because of the free admission concede that many are indeed interested in the further existence of the Gesellschaft. First Dr. Margolis, the leading literary/dramatic critic of the Chicago Jewish press spoke, and then I appealed for subscriptions. About ninety signed up, but whether they will actually pay their $3, $5 or $10 remains a question.

My position in the Gesellschaft remains about the same. That is, when they come up with a guarantee for me, I will start working for them. My one demand is that, if and when we have to leave America, we receive no less than $5,000. But if my plans regarding the Yiddish Dramatishe Gesellschaft and the Institute's English-language dramatic group materialize, we might have even more than that.

Of course, the whole scheme hangs on a thread. But I foresee a good outcome. Though nothing is settled, the work is progressing. The *Ger Tsedek* script is complete. Your role, Nehemella, now has flesh and blood. The play now has a new slant. The young duke is no longer just a mere strawman, but one who projects the true, beautiful idea of Judaism.

For the English-language group I have prepared David Pinsky's one-acter, *Dollar*. I plan to present it as a broad satire next month, August 25. From them I receive my salary with great respect, and have managed to save $150.

I have little to write about myself. I am feeling not bad. I rise early and work all day, trying hard to keep busy. I took a few English lessons with Miss Shapiro. I browse in books from the city library, and see only few people. I miss you, because there is nobody else who can get close to a wild creature like me.

When I see that things are not moving, I get gloomy, not so much for myself as for you. And I have been plagued by the thought that I do not do enough for you—something you have let me sense in your own subtle and refined fashion. But sensitive people like me experience the bite of a fly as if it were the sting of a wasp.

I want you to understand and not to be hurt by my words. It never occurred to me that I do not think enough about you. The truth is that I only think about matters that present a problem for me. And I never

Poster from Joseph Buloff's production of A. Kacyzne's Ger Tsedek (Convert), *St. Louis, 1929, with Buloff and Luba Kadison.*

considered you to be a problem in my life. I experience you as something as intrinsically natural to me as are my breath and heartbeat—always with me and hardly ever thought about.

You urge me to speak about myself despite my reluctance. But you are the only person who can relieve my depression. I admittedly remain a sickly child fond of playing in mud puddles, and it is you—my wife, my sister—who must wipe my dirty face.

Yet, believe me, never for a moment do I forget that you yourself are an artist and must meet the standards that your artistic nature requires. Yesterday I did think a great deal about you, because I began to miss you the moment you left. That was why I wrote to you that I wish to live my 120 years beside you, in any circumstances.

As I said, I see but few people, mostly because I have not sought to see anybody. My routine consists of going from home to the Institute in the morning and from the Institute home in the evening. Itkin, the actor, stays overnight with me a few nights a week. He sends regards. A very nice guy.

All who know you send regards. All tell me that they love you. But more than anybody, I love you. More than all those who will whisper in your ear that they are in love with you.

Buloff

To Leib Kadison in New York:

Chicago, 1928

Dear Kadison,

I have not written to you lately, because what more can I say to you than what Luba has already told you? There have been very few changes here. All the same, since your promise to send me news has aroused my curiosity,★ I will now write you a full letter.

I had almost decided to return to New York after our awards evening, even though Luba was hesitant. She is generally more optimistic than I am and, willing as she was to try another season in Chicago, she kept hoping for a miracle that would allow us to continue in the Dramatishe Gesellschaft. I, for my part, had no faith in such a possibility. Enthusiasm among our backers had declined. The Gesellschaft had used up its limited resources. So what was the use of beating a dead horse?

The actors were unwilling to give up. But for Luba and me, the issue was more complex. To continue working without a guarantee would be sheer madness. To reply on the promise that all efforts would be made to secure a guarantee was just as crazy. Therefore I concluded that we had come to the end of our Chicago venture.

Then something happened that opened new prospects and made the chance of our carrying on with our work in Chicago more realistic. As you know, the Jewish People's Institute—which owns the theatre and has been exacting an exorbitant rental from us—supports a troupe of English-language actors as well. It employs a director for them who thus far, from envy, has persecuted us. He also served as supervisor of the theatre, never allowing his actors to attend our Yiddish performances and constantly warning them that listening to Yiddish ruins the purity of their English.

★ Kadison's news concerned a possible re-establishment of the Vilna Troupe in New York.

However, a few of his players did sneak into our performances and, excited over what they had seen, informed their fellow players. Then they all came to our last presentations, as a result of which a conspiracy was hatched against the director—that old, worn-out theatre mouse. Although he was firmly entrenched in the job, the cast resolved to oust him. The troupe invited me to a private home and proposed that I collaborate with them on a studio piece, with which to open the trustees' eyes, and thus to instill myself as director.

Since my season with the Dramatishe Gesellschaft was over and there was no more work in that department, I agreed. They wanted to do a Yiddish play, specifically *The Dybbuk*. After several rehearsals, I clearly saw that *The Dybbuk* was too much for a group that knew less about Hassidic lore than we do about Sherlock Holmes mystery stories. But suddenly I had an idea. Having observed that they enjoyed singing Yiddish songs though they hardly understood the lyrics, I decided to do with them a revue★ of good old Jewish folksongs. I had the songs translated into English, and I staged the revue. It turned out to be just what we needed.

Shortly thereafter, I received an offer for a position with the Jewish People's Institute of Chicago. The old director had resigned.

The Institute proposed to pay me $75 per week through the summer, that is, until September, for producing a one-acter with a few cast members. In September I am to embark on serious work, with a raise in salary to $100 per week and a one-year contract.

Luba and I carefully considered the situation and came to a decision: We will concentrate more on English and perhaps that will solve all our damned problems.

But as you know, we still carry the old Yiddish burden. Our sentiment for our language, coupled with the uncertainty about citizenship, was preventing us from growing overly enthusiastic, until we worked out the following plan: We will use the Institute's proposal to serve the interests of the Yiddish Dramatishe Gesellschaft, and we will go on with Yiddish work within the Gesellschaft even as I satisfy the Institute's expectations with English-language productions. (A tall order to fill!)

On learning about my agreement with the Institute, the Gesellschaft took on a new life. At the same time, we received a proposal from Maurice Schwartz. You will understand why I responded coolly; I now have a position that satisfies me—spiritually and financially.

I am now the boss of the theatre. I come and go as I please. Formerly, I was admitted into the theatre only two hours before a performance. Now I occupy the largest office in the building, and I have nothing to do, because all the members are away in the country. Meanwhile, I am revising *The Dukus* (or *Ger Tsadek*)—a clumsy play, as you know, but I got tired of looking for something else, went to work on *Dukus*, and in seven weeks made something worthwhile out of it.

That is all the news from Chicago. I am glad I wrote, because now you will feel obligated to give me all the news of New York.

Buloff

★ *The Rainbow*, a folksong revue, which Buloff presented successfully in Chicago and in New York.

Farewell to Chicago

After a refreshing summer spent with my sister at a Catskill resort, I returned to Chicago for the second season. When it ended, Buloff and I agreed it was time to return to the professional theatre. To be sure, the Yiddish Dramatishe Gesellschaft had given Buloff an opportunity to do experimental work, and he had succeeded in transplanting the language and style of the Vilna Troupe to American soil. Moreover, his work with the English-language dramatic group of the Jewish People's Institute of Chicago had given him a start towards the American theatre.

But we had to face the fact that the part-time amateur performers in our two troupes would never grow into professionals. We ourselves were not progressing as actors. And, finally, the impending expiration of our temporary visas was forcing us to seek professional employment in order to finance our return to Europe. Buloff wrote the following letter from New York to the Gesellschaft's manager in Chicago:

July 4, 1929

Dear Mason:

I hardly know how to answer your letter, for I have no concrete news. I know you would prefer some real news about us, but it will be days before anything is settled here.

I, too, would like to have some real news from you in Chicago, but I know that the situation there is confused.

In a few weeks I will have to apply again for a visa extension, and I will need a contract and $1,000 for the purpose. I can get an agreement, but in order to borrow $1,000, I must have a firm offer from a producer of a theatre company. The man who lent me the bond money in Chicago the first time will not do it this time, I am afraid.

While I expect to have the matter of a contract straightened out in ten days, the application for an extension cannot be delayed even one day. That means that I must decide before long whether or not to come to Chicago.

It is useless to keep going over the same thing. There is no better place for Yiddish theater than Chicago. It may not be perfect, but at least it offers an opportunity to do real theatre which is not possible in New York. Here, you have to take big chances, present big productions. And right now, unfortunately, I see very little chance to put on something serious that would compare to the work we produced in Chicago.

The Yiddish Theatre in New York has been poisoned. Mediocrity reigns as crowned king and the masses worship its standard low-brow fare. Nowhere is *Di Vilde Moid* (*The Wild Maiden*, a cheap melodrama) received with such delight as on Second Avenue.

On the other hand, some changes do seem to be occurring on the local stage. There is a sense of an impending earth tremor, and rumor has it that the Yiddish Theatre might yet rise to a higher standard, even if for the time being things still remain as they are.

We must recognize that New York is a city that loves to be surprised, while it itself never ceases to amaze. I have always maintained that the Yiddish Theatre lives on miracles; and New York City can produce more miracles than Chicago.

Therefore, if I consider staying in New York, I must be prepared to turn myself into a magician, which would make me very weary, for I prefer to be a plain artisan.

Let me tell you frankly, I feel crushed. The strongest tree is the one that bends with the wind, but I choose never to bend. You are familiar with my perseverance and strength, yet two or three heavy blows can put a hole right through my heart.

And such a hole, I think, can be repaired only by the local Vilna Troupe.

The Vilner are cursed by God, like the Eternal Jew. May they live forever, as he does. They were drowned so many times, but each time the water rejected them. They were burned again and agin, and did not go up in smoke. So often it looked as if they already had departed for the next world, but when a testing feather brushed against their nose, they sneezed and lived again. Long life to them!

The Vilna Troupe is like the legendary snake. Cut it to pieces and each piece gets a life of its own. In spite of the world, in spite of itself.

Now the New York Vilner wish to mobilize, with me, Buloff, as their general. But how does one fight a war without ammunition?

When members of the theatrical fraternity ask, "So, Buloff, what are you going to do next season?" I answer, "I am going back to Chicago." But deep in my heart, I know that I will be acting this coming fall in New York.

Read this letter to my friends and let them know I greet them. Luba sends regards, too.

Yours,
Buloff

Thoughts of returning to Europe were expressed by Buloff in a letter to his aging father:

New York

Dear Father:

It has been two weeks since I heard about your operation, but I waited for your letter before writing. Mother told me of it, then, in a second letter, tried to smooth it over, apparently, to spare me concern. She is always the good *mamelle* who smothers her own pain. So all I could do was wait for a letter from you.

You can imagine how impatiently I waited, and when your letter arrived, how my heart pounded as I opened it. Even as I read about your unfortunate circumstances in Vilna, I found comfort in the news that you are full of courage and hope.

Although your letter sounds rather like a will, it shows that you have not lost your sense of humor.

How lucky I am that I am part of you, that I possess the same stubbornness that never allows you to fall down, even when an angry fate thrusts upon your shoulders a weight of a thousand pounds.

What can I say? I really don't know. You think it might be a good idea for me to abandon the stage and turn to business. Let me tell you: If

Copy of page from Joseph Buloff's letter to his father; from notebook in which Buloff recorded copies of his correspondence.

I were capable of being as good a businessman as I am an actor, it would have already naturally happened. But unfortunately, I would make a very poor businessman.

Don't think that one cannot do business in the theatre. Yet even in the theatre I am a weak operator. So you can imagine how successful I would be selling brushes.

A person is born to his profession. Maybe acting is not a profession, but one is born to be an actor, and one must live and die as such. A man cannot separate himself from himself.

Suppose that Buloff the man were to say to Buloff the actor: "Listen, good brother, leave me alone and go away in good health! And

Buloff the merchant will start a business." Do you suppose the actor and the businessman would do just that? The actor in me would knock out all my teeth, so that even if the businessman brought me food, I would be unable to chew or digest it.

Now, the fact that on top of everything I am a Yiddish actor makes for heartbreak. But that is not entirely my fault. Your name is Benjamin, not Nikolai the Russian or Jim the American.

The fact remains that I am an inept businessman, and this I cannot change. But since I am only twenty-eight years old, I might still change Joseph to Jefferson.★ It is up to God.

In any event, I can assure you that lots of businessmen, craftsmen, lawyers and even doctors envy me. As for your warning that an old actor is worse than an apostate, and that someday I will grow old, it does not worry me. First of all, I refuse to think about growing old. Tell me, is an old banker worth more than a spit in the sea?

No, dear father, I am determined to stay young—as young as you are in spirit. You have had a hard life, suffered disease, bore heavy family responsibilities, and now you face one operation after another. Yet you write your name with pride: Benjamin Buloff.

Furthermore, dear father, you must know that in large part you are responsible for my having become an actor, for it was you who used to smear my face with soot and put me up on the table to recite Othello's monologue. Besides, deep down, you yourself have always been a bit of an actor, and since my earliest childhood I have tried to model myself on you. Today, when I appear onstage, in many of my roles, I embody you— your huge Don Quixote mustaches, your high pitches, your naive enthusiasms for the fantastic, your courage in coping with war wounds, your talent for your craft,★★ your folksy humor, your tragicomic spirit. Something of these I have inherited from you, and when I create character parts on stage, I mirror you.

As you lie in pain now, far from me, shattered by the heavy blows that fate has dealt you, I want you to know that never for one moment did I forget you. With all my being I am you.

You say that in the event the scalpel slips, your estate is in order and you are leaving me your old truss. To this I reply that no man can inherit greater wealth: Your brave humor, despite pain, despite misfortune, is the finest literature that I have read in all my years. How I relish your depictions of your morning activities as you take your teeth out of the cabinet, bind up your double hernia, clear out the fragments of lungs that your damned asthma has left you, brush your mighty mustache, and go out to kid the girls. I treasure your letters as my Torah. What more can a son want from a father?

Your admonition that I not forget your wife and children, I accept as the Law. For surely you know that your wife and children are my mother and sisters. I am confident that from all the operations and tribulations you will emerge well and strong. But rest assured that in all the confusions of the world, the only holiness that I have preserved from my childhood is my mother—the little mother who walked in torn shoes through winter frosts from Chirvent to Vilna with a loaf of bread hidden in her bosom.

★ He did not change his name. On the American (non-Yiddish) stage, he retained the name with which he was born.
★★ He was a master furrier.

Have no fear! Your life will be saved. The question of whether I should continue to be an actor, or how I would support Mother are not important now. What is important is for you to gather all your strength and summon the will to conquer the pain that is tormenting you.

I am making plans to come to Europe to see you. By my next letter, I hope to be able to tell you when I start out.

Be well. Luba sends you all the blessings in the world.

Your son,
Joseph

The Vilna Troupe in the Bronx

The 1930 theatre season found us back in New York City, where we made one more effort to revive the American wing of the Vilna Troupe. With Buloff, Leib Kadison and me as the nucleus, the company added Rose Jalasow, Leah Naomi, Tanin, Wolf Barzel, Vera Niraslovaska, Moishe Feder and Lubetsky. Abe Feder, the lighting expert, and Ziporin, the stage designer, came from Chicago to help. We rented a shabby theatre on 149th Street in the Bronx and presented *Periphery*, *Ger Tsedek*, *School Friends*, and *The Rainbow*, a musical revue.

On the artistic level we were quite successful. Maurice Schwartz made the long trip from Second Avenue to see our *Ger Tsedek* and was impressed. *The Rainbow* elicited from the critic of the Yiddish literary weekly *Fraye Arbeter Shtime* (*Free Voice of Labor*) the comment that anyone wishing to enjoy true Yiddish Theatre would do well to travel to the Bronx.

Joseph Buloff and Luba Kadison in the musical revue The Rainbow, *New York, 1930.*

Poster from The Rainbow.

However, troubles beset our Vilna Troupe. We could not afford union stagehands, and the attempt to operate as a non-unionized house provoked reprisals from the powerful stagehands union. Stench bombs were hurled during our performances. We would open the doors, ventilate the theatre and go on with the production; but the distraction was always painful.

Because of such disruptions and especially because of our theatre's inconvenient location, we scored poorly at the box office. Joe and I were earning about $15 a week for endless, backbreaking labor. At the end of the season, we abandoned all effort to revive the Vilna Troupe in New York.

During our season in the Bronx, Buloff wrote to Mazo in Vilna.

New York
March 1931

Dear friend Mazo,

I was happy when I received what I thought was a letter from you. But imagine my disappointment when I tore open the envelope and found only a statement of theatre expenses. I realized what had happened: in error, you had slipped into the envelope the account instead of your letter.

I am still puzzled, however, because I do not know for a fact that the envelope was indeed sent by you. The return address on it is that of a Dr. Bigotski, yet the handwriting and the voucher inside seem to be yours. Since you might need the paper for your records, I am mailing it back.

I am very eager to hear from you. Your present situation interests me greatly. We receive fragments of news about you from time to time, but I do not have a clear idea about your work. How long will you spend in Vilna? What are your future plans? Who are the actors in the Troupe? In general, how are you and Orleska?

Our U.S. permit expires this year, and we will have to leave no later than the end of April. I cannot tell you how painful this will be for me, and I am therefore trying with all my powers to void the order. But the chances are slim, and we will probably be back in Europe before long.

As I sit here writing, Silberzweig, editor of the Lexicon, walks in with the news that you are about to celebrate the 15th anniversary of the Vilna Troupe. Could it be that instead of the account slip you meant to mail me an announcement and an invitation?

If so, heartfelt thanks! For the occasion, I would like to prepare a special greeting to the banquet guests, but I fear that it might arrive too late, for Silberzweig informs me that the celebration is scheduled for March 15. On that day, Luba and I will drink to your health, to the health of our old colleagues and that of the new actors who, with you, are carrying on the traditions of the Vilna Troupe.

Yours,
Luba and Buloff

THE NEW YORK TIMES, SUNDAY, NOVEMBER 23, 1930.

INTRODUCING JOSEPH BULOFF OF RUSSIA

By WILLIAM SCHACK.

HE is only in his early 30s; he has been in this country only a few years; yet it is hardly extravagant to acclaim Joseph Buloff as the most gifted actor on the Yiddish stage in America and his reappearance on Second Avenue with the Yiddish Art Theatre as the outstanding event of its season. And it is an event for the non-Jewish public as well, for Buloff is one of those mimes who, penetrating their rôles with such finesse that they become not only the spirit but the body of their characters, break down the barriers of language and give to their art something of the universality of the dance.

It is always art with Buloff, never the raw exploitation of his personality. If any single performance were not proof enough that he does not play himself but is always absorbed by his rôle, then his career as a whole would bear out the fact; for in the brief dozen years he has been on the stage he has created some seventy parts, ranging from the simple buffoon through sharply individualized comic and tragic characters to the hierarchic dignitary which is his rôle in a current offering of the Maurice Schwartz troupe.

* * *

Playing as he does with an ensemble well above the average, Buloff nevertheless sometimes makes them seem lifeless puppets, standing stock still by contrast with his constant mobility of body and mind. If this were merely the rapacious reaching out for attention of a "star," it would of course be damaging to the performance as a whole; but one is instantly aware that here is no strutting vulgarian but a man obsessed by the demon of his art, surpassing the others only because he has surrendered himself so much more completely. One can measure his creative ability admirably in "The Witch of Castile." In the first place, he is cast as a Pope persecuting the Jews—a rôle few Jewish actors, however broadminded, could undertake with equanimity. Buloff himself thought it would elicit a hostile response from the audience, so that he made preparations for possible interruptions. But even this unsympathetic rôle he invests with such glamour that he transmutes the hatred his audience would feel for this character in the flesh to admiration for his effigy in art. In the second place, the play itself is of the sluggish historical sort, with the actors finding little nourishment in the text out of which to build living

characters. Buloff's is really the only three-dimensional breathing figure; without more text to go by than the others, his creation of the character of the Pope out of himself is therefore the more striking.

To see him next in one of the troupe's repertory, "The God of Vengeance" of Sholom Asch, is to witness a startling transformation. Here, as Reb Elyeh, as the man who will get you a wife or a husband, or straighten things out for you with the rabbi, or with God himself—even if you are, as in this play, a brothel keeper—he makes the audience gape and wriggle with a delighted astonishment that—the more amazing since his is a comic rôle—approaches ecstasy. When Reb Elyeh makes his first entrance, doing the honors for the rabbi whose factotum he is, it is like a tornado, and, since he never relents, when he sweeps off the stage a vacuum is momentarily left behind before the others can rush in and fill it. As Buloff plays him, making use of all the gestures Jews ever have used or ever can use, you realize that Reb Elyeh does not work for money but because he was born to bring together, to negotiate, to be a go-between, the eternal "fixer." Buloff makes him, not a type, but the summation of a type.

The rich background of observation which underlies his imaginative interpretations of Jewish character, Buloff acquired in Russia and Poland. His first venture on the stage was in the Jewish State Theatre which the Russians established in Vilna in 1918 after the German Army of occupation had withdrawn. From there he went to Lodz, an important Polish centre. When the Polish Army invaded Russia in 1922, he was taken prisoner, and so smelled the inside of his third barracks, for he had joined the Russian Army when he was just out of school and later had been captured and made to serve as interpreter to the German victors. When peace was concluded, the Poles did him a good turn by releasing him in Warsaw, where the Vilna Truppe was then at the height of its fame.

* * *

Buloff was taken on by this company, but soon the military and political squabbles of the region were reinforced by theatrical ones. There were factions in the Vilna Truppe. It had perfected a minutely realistic art against which some of its younger members, Buloff included, were in rebellion. In the meantime, however, touring Austria and Poland, he was learning what he could from the older men and from the

villages which are the source of Jewish life as we know it today. In one of these villages, when the company put on "The Dybbuk," black candles were lit in the synagogue and the actors excommunicated.

When the Vilna Truppe split up, Buloff took one unit to Rumania. There he scored two striking successes -- in the Messianic play "Shabtai Zvi" and in Dymov's "The Singer of His Sorrow." The latter ran for 300 successive performances in Bucharest, with another 100 thrown in at odd times later, creating such a stir that, whatever pogroms may have preceded and followed it, the King himself sent in his card to this lowly Jewish theatre asking that seats be reserved for his party.

* * *

In 1926 Maurice Schwartz brought Buloff to New York for a short season. He did not fail to attract attention, but there were difficulties and, as a result, Buloff moved on to Chicago the next year. For two seasons he engaged in tremendous activity there, directing both a Yiddish and an English theatre. In both he carried on experiments with that stylization which, already in his first stage days in Vilna, had seemed preferable to him to a petty realistic treatment, although there is a soundly realistic basis to his work. His Yiddish group in Chicago put on no less than ten plays, and the English theatre half as many, including Hirschbein's "The Haunted Inn," Pinsky's "The Dollar" and a Jewish revue (in English). His work with the latter group was especially valuable in giving him the feel of a language which he hopes to use as his medium at not too distant a date.

Last season he directed a small theatre in the Bronx, obscure so far as the general public and even most of the cognoscenti were concerned. From it, however, several individuals brought back glowing accounts. His crowning achievement there was his production of the Czech Langer's "Periphery" (under the title "Mord"), which elicited high critical praise. Among his other productions were Ludwig Fulda's "The Old Bachelors" and another revue, a series of dramatizations of Jewish folksongs.

Buloff is to direct certain of the Schwartz plays this season. Whether as director or as actor alone, in the new or repertory plays which are given the first half of the week, it is worth traveling much further than Second Avenue to see him; for even if he should appear on Broadway next year, it is opportunity lost not to witness the work of this admirable actor before then.

Clipping from The New York Times, *November 23, 1930, with story on Joseph Buloff.*

Back to Bucharest

Even if our Bronx venture had been more successful, we could not have continued it. The dreaded moment came—the expiration of all visa extensions. We had to return to Europe. Fortunately, we found a temporary haven when Sandow—a Rumanian impresario backed by the wealthy clothing manufacturer Perelman—invited us to return to the scene of some of our greatest triumphs, Bucharest.

Leib and Chanah Kadison accompanied us, and Sandow also imported a few other experienced actors from Warsaw, including Mr. and Mrs. David Licht and Mr. and Mrs. Mansdorf. (David Licht later came to the United States and became the director of the still active Folksbiene Theatre.)

We opened with *Periphery* and then presented *The Rainbow*, *The Kibbitzer* by Jo Swerling and Edward G. Robinson (as adapted and translated into Yiddish by Buloff), *Samson and Delilah*, and *The Dybbuk*. The season proved to be a replay of our 1920's successes in Rumania. The press, Yiddish and Rumanian alike, had high praise for Buloff and acclaimed us as "The Return of the Vilna Troupe." Audiences flocked to our performances. At the beginning, we used the beautiful Regina

On tour in Rumania: Bucharest, 1931. Left to right: A. Sandow; Luba Kadison; Joseph Buloff; Chanah Kadison; I. Sternberg; Leib Kadison.

NUMAR GRATUIT

Joi 9 Iulie 1931

Redacţia şi Administraţia la TEATRUL NOU Cal. Văcăreşti Nr. 34

CRONICA TEATRALA

Apare sub auspiciile direcţiunei **I. Sternberg** şi **A. Samuelly-Sandu** — Secretar, A. Schönfeld

Presa Capitalei despre artistul IOSIF BULOW în CHIBIŢUL

Dimineaţa 30 Iunie

Teatrele de vară

BULOW

Impresiile tari impun tăcere. Astfel, confidenţa ajunge a fi simţită ca o profanare; cu atât mai mult confidenţa publică.

Dacă n'ar fi întrebările inevitabile ale prietenilor, poate că nici în cerc intim nu aş vorbi despre Bulow. Cred că nu l-am aplaudat niciodată; frumuseţea acţiunii lui imobilizează.

Insă acumularea unor impresii de calitatea celor pe cari ni le dă arta acestui tânăr, sparge, dela un timp cătuşele admiraţiei mute. Atunci vine vremea să strigi în gura mare.

Este un semn al plăcerii rafinate, că ea te farmecă şi te lasă nesatisfăcut. E sentimentul că te afli înaintea unui izvor ce nu se istoveşte, de lângă care ai vrea să nu mai pleci.

Aseară, când perdeaua s'a lăsat pentru a închide actul din urmă al CHIBIŢULUI, am rămas pe scaun aşteptând, parcă, să înceapă jocul din capăt. Aceeaşi sete mi-a lăsat-o ori ce sfârşit de reprezentaţie, la Bulow. După comedia de care vorbesc, impresia de nesăturare infinită e poate mai violentă, fiindcă pe Bulow îl avem, aici, aproape tot timpul în scenă.

In omul acesta trăieşte un extraordinar demon artistic; lângă demon un maistru: o inteligenţă neadormită, un gust de continuă severitate, o discreţie estetică de o siguranţă pe care ai evalua-o în fracţiuni de milimetru, infime.

Să spunem simplu: Bulow este o minune de fantezie caşi de virtuozitate dramatică. Agitaţia delicioasă care e efectul propriu al acestei arte de mişcare eminent umană, nu cred să o mai fi simţit, în teatru, la aşa grad de ascuţime. In unele momente, ea e ca o durere voluptoasă, amestec de simţiri spre cari tinde, pare că, esenţa însăşi a fiinţei noastre, şi de care ai vrea să nu aibă sfârşit. Instinctul e aici abilitate supremă; simţurile sunt inteligenţă care scapără. Bulow este o explicaţie vie a ceea ce e arta; vreau să zic: realizarea deplină a ceea ce, de obiceiu ea vrea, să fie.

Toate aceste nu sunt decât constatări elementare ale unor impresii ce se impun imediat. Exprimarea lor nu e fără oarecare amărăciune, la care e predestinat criticul; fiindcă nu poţi uita mulţimea acelor ce nu iau seama destul, pentru a deosebi pe un Bulow de un abil oarecare.

Vă amintiţi bine încovoiarea spinării şi răguşeala bunicii care împleteşte ciorap şi spune nepoatei povestea CÂNTĂREŢULUI TRISTEŢII SALE? Sau intonaţiile judecătorului de instrucţie — un amănunt şi mai episodic încă — în CADAVRUL VIU? — Locul lui Bulow poate fi în centrul spectacolului sau oricât de lateral, frumuseţea jocului său păstrează aceiaşi superioritate. Imparţialitatea artistului e ca şi a naturii; iar nouă, modernilor, pentru care primadona şi primul amorez sunt funcţiuni degradate şi anulate, ne este cu deosebire scump un artist atât de curat de parţialitatea grosolană a celor ce nu sunt decât cabotini abili.

Inălţimea însăşi pe care se află creaţia artistică a lui Bulow, îi permite acea stranie egalitate de măestrie în figuri atât de diverse ca ŞAPSAI ZWI CHIBIŢ, CÂNTĂREŢUL TRISTEŢEI SALE... In toate, energia lui inventivă este la maximum, în absoluă libertate.

Verva sa mimică şi verbală îţi taie răsuflarea. Atenţia e perpetuu însetată' deşi necontenit saturată. Detaliul jocului său este o bogăţie zdrobitoare totuşi virtuozitatea desăvârşită îi dă siguranţă instinctivă de a doza; o clipă măcar nu încetează impresia de a fi armonică.

CHIBIŢUL e o comedie de construcţie tradiţională, cu excelent meşteşug lucrată; teatru pur, pe care nici o ambiţie literară, sau altfel lăturalnică, nu-l alterează. Un personaj primează, învie şi întreţine jocul celorlalţi. El se află în afect continuu; replicele celorlalţi se orientează discret în jurul acţionării şi debitului său, ce funcţionează aproape ca un monolog. In susţinerea unui asemenea exces de acţiune, Bulow atinge marginile ultime ale energiei artistice. Este o risipă rafinată de invenţiune în gest şi în rostire, de care nu poţi şti cum poate încânta la aşa potenţă, fără a-ţi obosi măcar o secundă tensiunea delicioasă a spiritului.

Exaltarea lucidă proprie artei dionizice. nu-mi amintesc să o mai fi simţit realizată atât de întreg ca în jocul aceetui om de teatru.

Şi este cu neputinţă ca, sub focul jocului său, partenerii să poate rămâne vreodată un ansamblu slab. Despre talentul şi ştiiţa domnului Sternberg, nimic nou nu pot întreprinde a spune cunoscătorilor, eu care nu vorbesc de arta teatrului decât ca un om din public.

PAUL ZARIFOPOL

CHIBIŢUL Actul III

Arta lui Bulow

Ca şi în dramele şi tragediile lui, teatrul lui Bulow ţine, şi'n comedie, sa fie teatru pentru elită.

Chiar când vrea să amuze publicul cu totdinadinsul, el nu-i va da piesa care să-l facă să se ţie cu mâinile de burtă derâs, adică nu-i va da un teatru popular „bon enfant" ci o comedie fină cu adânci scrutări psichologice, cu întrupări detipuri şi caractere care, chiar când sunt comice te fac rar să râzi cu poftă — un râs fizic, — ci mai mult să surâzi.

Surâsul e doar caracteristic omului.

De râs, râd şi unele animale.

Deşi joacă pe o scenă improvizată dintr'o grădină de cartier, Bulow inobilează locul prin marea sa personalitate artistică.

In toate acele scene prinse „sur le vif" din „Chibiţul" în acea infinită frământare sufletească exteriorizată prin aparentul nasfârşit monolog, care, debitat de un artist mediocru ar fi devenit plictisitor, puternicul talent dramatic al lui Bulow nu te părăseşte o clipă şi te ţine captivat de fiecare gest şi de fiecare cuvânt rostit de el.

In personajul pe care-l creiază Bulow inobilează locul prin marea sa moria şi sesnibilitatea sa au înregistrat spontan în subconştient, din impresiile culese ochiul lui pătrunzător din toate ambianţele sociale.

Subiectul piesei? Dar subiectul e un suflet pitoresc şi original pe care-l întrupează eroul: Lazăr „Chibiţul". Să notăm întâi mediul din care răsare eroul pe care ni-l înfăţişează Bulow. E getto-ul newyorkez. In acest getto un simplu debit de ţigări, în care-şi trăeşte Bulow (Lazăr) viaţa sa agitată continuu de un singur ideal, de o singură patimă, de o monomanie, mania jocurilor de bazard, a jocului de cărţi, de bursă, etc.

El nu joacă fiindcă n'are para chioară, dar ia parte cu întreaga lui fiinţă, la delirul tuturor celor cuprinşi de patima jocului. Face să vii să vezi arta cu care Bulow exteriorizează fiecare vibrare a sufletului, cu artă atât de fină că uiţi că eşti la teatru şi crezi în spontaneitatea fiecărui gest şi a fiecărui cuvânt.

In artn lui Bulow nu e atât fantezia, cât ingenioasa şi pitorească abilitate de a şti să scoată din cele mai neînsemnate evenimente cele mai fericite efecte şi să stoarcă dintr'o situaţie tot comicul ce conţine, făcând să ţâşnească la timp cuvântul sau gestul ce te sileşte să pufneşti de râs.

DOCTORUL YGREC

Adevărul 1 Iulie

I. Bulow în Chibiţul

FALSĂ CRONICA DRAMATICA

BULOW SAU DĂ-MI UN MĂR...

de F. ADERCA

Iosef Bulow, evreu originar din Polonia unde a dobândit educaţie şi cultură rusească, cunoscut din România unde a fost protagonistul în idiş al unor spectacole de supremă artă dramatică şi de curând artist de limbă engleză la New-York, e mai mult decât un interpret. Merge până la deformarea sau — ca să întrebuinţăm o expresie mai dulce — până la adaptarea sufletească a eroului pe măsura insuşirilor scenice ale artistului. Fenomenul se petrece cu toţi marii artişti, o sonată de Mozart devenind sub arcuşul lui Enescu o sonată de Enescu - Mozart iar o piesă de Frantisec Langer un spectacol Bulow - Langer. Piesa scrisă e un lucru în sine, piesa reprezentată e alt lucru în sine. Se vor putea indigna muzicografii pe Backhaus pentru felul în care'l redă pe Beethoven sau literaţii pentru deteriorarea la care Bulow a supus eroul scriitorului ceh — preschimbând un ins de o rară gingăşie sufletească, criminal din întâmplare şi fără voe, într'un criminal furios — toate aceste indignări dovedesc numai că n'au făcut distincţiile necesare.

Eroul lui Frantisec Langer (Franţi din „Periferie") a fost întrupat odată şi de un tânăr viguros actor de la noi care, mult mai credincios textului a izbutit să realizeze un flăcău patetic şi de inimă aleasă. Mult mai complex a fost Bulow. El a văzut în derbedeul de mahala în primul rând un personagiu comic care poartă în sine un suflet de o tragică înălţime. Bulow a cumulat — ca să luăm termeni de comparaţie dela noi şi dintre contemporani — pentru a realiza pe *Franţi* din „Periferie". mimica şi fantezia (duse până la meticulos) a lui Iancovescu şi nebunia grava şi inconştient sublimă a lui Morţun (din „Raţa sălbatecă" de Ibsen sau din orice piesă de Tolstoi). Verva înfrigurată cu care *tace*, învăluit în nouri de fum ai unui muc de trabuc, spre a mărturisi camarazilor în scurte hohote de râs că a făcut moarte de om sau povestea *mută* a asasinatului în pivniţa marelui judecător utopic, sunt creaţii unice. Mâinile lui Bulow, care arată că las'n urma lui, jos, pe scânduri, un hoit omenesc, scuturătură abia perceptibilă şi spasmodică a degetelor ca de un vis de care ar vreai să se scape şi înţepenirea lor, ca leşul după spasmele din urmă, vin de-adreptul din talmudul halucinant.

L'am întrebat pe d. I. Sternberg, poetul şi regisorul, între colonade e Teatrului Regina Maria, după spectacol:

— De ce n'a rămas Bulow în România?.. Nu l'a văzut nici unul din numeroşii noştri oameni

Cronica Teatrală

TEATRUL NOU: „Chibiţul", comedie în 3 acte de Rabinsohn

Chibiţul e tipul prin natura lui enervant. Iţi stă nepoftit la spate sau la coastă, şi are păreri pe care le debitează cu exuberantă volubilitate.

Simţul critic îi es'e desvoltat, superdesvoltat. Fiecare gest sau chiar intenţie a ta, prinse în cleştele observaţiei sale analitice, a disectat cu o voluptoasă cruzime.

Dar nu atât cruzimea sa e supărătoare, cât lipsa oricărei sensibilităţi auto-critice.

Emfaza superiorităţii şi aerul de a toate ştiutor şi prevăzător pe care şi-l ia chibiţul, — socotinduse astfel în drept să te cicălească şi chiar să te muştruluiască — îl face nesuferit.

Pune în locul tău pe omul care te sâcâie cu comentariile sale când joci cărţi şi vei vedea că el joacă mai prost ca tine. Aceasta nu-l va împiedica însă, ca atunci când a revenit pe fotoliul chibiţului, să discute şi să găsească pointa critică a jocului tău.

Un astfel de tip, nervos, vorbăreţ şi cicălitor l-a inspirat pe americanul Robinsohn să scrie comedia „Chibiţul". Dar autorul nu sa oprit la fixarea unul obişnuit chibiţ de cafenea, ci l-a umanizat, i-a dat proporţii şi ni l-a înfăţişat ca un veritabil chibiţ al jocului care e viaţa însăşi.

Pe acest chibiţ, Robinsohn ni l-a prezentat în cadrul prielnic al neamului evreesc din cartierele New-Yorkului, unde majoritatea trăeşte în legănarea visului de subită ascensiune, graţie unei lovituri la curse, la bursă sau la loterie.

Mediul evreesc e minunat redat, cu pitorescul lui vizual, cu humorul specific rasei, cu acea sociabilitate care micşorează distanţele dintre oameni.

„Chibiţul" însă pe lângă acest caracter pictural, mai are şi o uşoară tinctură satirică, evidenţiată în final. Ca să câştigi la bursă nu-ţi trebue inteligenţă, ci norocul prostului. Chibiţul Lazăr dă lovitura care-l îmbogăţeşte, graţie răspunsului întâmplător afirmativ prin telefon, ai fratelui său cretin, care nu poate îngâna decât trei cuvinte: Da, desigur, fireşte.

Comedia a fost îngrijit montată pe scena Teatrului Nou, şi s'a desfăşurai într'un ritm viu şi antrenat. D. Iosif Bulow a făcut o frumoasă creaţie în rolul chibiţului Lazăr. A izbutit să evidenţieze caracteristicile personalului nervos obsedat de ideia îmbogăţirii repezi, volubil şi convingător, acidulat în judecată şi expresii, fără a fi corosiv însă. In deosebi a excelat în redarea acelei trepidaţii, care e specifică oamenilor cuprinşi de febra afacerilor.

Cu migăloasă artă d. Bulow a ştiut să dea coloratură comică rolului, în acea fină şi omenească tristeţă, care face farmecul interpretărilor d-sale. In dosul gesturilor sale comice, în miezul glumelor sale savuroase, mocneşte tragicul vieţei împovărate de griji, de belele şi împiedicată de neprevăzute obstacole în avântul ei ascensional.

Bulow n'a făcut din chibiţ o imagine bufă — rolul se preta atât de gras la aceasta — ci a schiţat o figură omenească şi profund impresionantă.

D-na **Liuba Kadison** *a avut momente emoţionante în rolul fiicei chibiţului, d. D. Licht a interpretat cu desinvoltură pe îndrăgostitul logodnic, iar d. Leo Kadison s'a prezentat cu prezenţa unui autentic bogătaş.*

Pe cretinul Iacob, ni l-e înfăţişat amuzant d. Sch. Schönbaum.

Ansamblul a fast complectat reuşit cu d-nele Rut Tharu, Ana Mogel, Miki Kahane şi d-nii I. Mansdorf, S. Bader. S. Weinstok, H. Gherschensohn.

Reprezentaţia, înflorită de râsetele spectatorilor, a fost aplaudată şi va face serie.

A. MUNTE

Dimineaţa 26 Iunie 1931

Theatre bulletin publicizing the Rumanian tour of Joseph Buloff, Luba Kadison and company, Bucharest, 1931.

Theatre, then our old open-air Zhitnetsa, and later took our plays to Jassy and Chernowitz.

Buloff wrote about our Rumanian season as follows:

Bucharest
1931

Dear Mazo,

I received your letter two days before we boarded ship, and I am therefore answering you from Bucharest, where Luba and I and Kadison and Chanah arrived a week ago.

I don't know where to start. It is impossible in a short letter to relate all the adventures, experiences and impressions stored up in the course of my five years in America.

It is quite likely that fate will soon bring us together again, and I will then be able to tell you, over a glass of tea, all about our past wanderings and future plans. Meanwhile, I can send you only greetings from this Rumanian land, where we have had success and joy. Here we are under a contract to Sandow. He is presenting our tour with great pride. How long we spend here depends on the American consul, but it is not inconceivable that on leaving Rumania we shall travel through Poland. It would be good if we could play with you for at least a month or two in some new productions.

Our reunion could be presented as part of the anniversary of the Vilna Troupe. If this stikes you as a good idea, please reply promptly— specifying where and when it could materialize. Let me also know your terms.

As I said, Leib and Chanah Kadison are with us in Rumania. The purpose of their trip was to go to Poland to see their son, Itzhak. Well, as long as they are in Europe, why not get into a few theatrical performances?

Regards from Luba and all to you and Orleska.

Yours,
Buloff

To Linder, a Yiddish writer for the New York *Morgen Journal*.

Bucharest
1931

Dear friend Linder:

Thank you for your warm letter. I must tell you the truth: Except for Mrs. Margoshes, who wrote us a short note, nobody has answered our letters as yet. Of our American friends, you two are the only ones to cheer us with a kind word.

Now let me describe our present situation. We were encouraged by the warm reception upon arrival in Bucharest. What a contrast between the welcome to Rumania and the gloomy farewell to New York!

Ten days have passed since our first appearance, and I already count twenty-two articles in the newspapers. More was written about us in the first ten days here than in all the five years we spent in America.

In Rumania, though I perform in Yiddish, I am recognized as a world actor. You can better understand the significance of what I am telling you when you realize that the public that comes to our theatre is thirty-five percent non-Jewish. As they say in America, so long as we make a living, the customer can be a Tartar, for all we care.

Thank God, we have made a few Dollars here—perhaps a temporary blessing, because in the final analysis, Yiddish Theatre is for Jews. And where in the world are there more Jews than in New York? No wonder then, that despite our good fortune here, we are still contemplating a return to New York. Of course—to paraphrase the old saying—"Man proposes, but the Ameican consul disposes."

As of now, his advice is to wait until July. Then he will see what he can do for us.

Let us hope that we will soon be sitting together over a glass of prohibition brew.

Buloff

Luba Kadison as Delilah in S. Lange's Samson and Delilah, *Bucharest, 1931.*

As reported by Buloff in his letter to Mazo, my parents also played parts in the plays. Father was a leading character actor and stage manager as well as designer. Leib and Chanah had another special reason for accompanying us to Europe. Word had reached them that their son, Itzhak, had returned to and was clandestinely living in Poland with a wife and a little daughter.

Joseph Buloff as the Rabbi in S. Ansky's Dybbuk, *Bucharest, 1931.*

As soon as their performance schedule permitted, they took the train from Bucharest to Warsaw, and Paula, who had come over for a holiday, joined them. They found Itzhak and his family hiding in a hut in the woods outside Warsaw. Although he was clad in rags, he showed them a large roll of cash, which the USSR had entrusted to him to smuggle in for the outlawed Polish Communist Party. He also showed his parents and sister a pistol that he carried to protect the Comintern's money from potential traitors.

The Kadisons embraced their long-lost son, his new wife, Zosia, and their first grandchild, Lenka, and returned to Bucharest. They never saw Itzhak again. He returned to Moscow with his wife and child.

Upon completion of his mission to Warsaw, he continued to correspond with us, and occasionally had his poems published in *The Freiheit*—the leftist New York daily—under the pen-name Itzhak Kovner.

But in 1936, letters from him abruptly stopped. We guessed all too accurately that, in one of the early Stalin purges, he and his wife had been arrested—and that is all we ever learned about their fate. We still do not know whether they were executed in Moscow or were sent to perish in the Gulag.

Their daughter, Lenka (named for Lenin), was placed in a school for children of political prisoners where she received the mandatory indoctrination, and when she reached her teens, she was released to live with a local Polish-Jewish family, friends of Itzhak's.

A few years later, the family was allowed to return to Warsaw (by then under Communist rule) with Lenka. She began to write to us. Her first letters were filled with the grief of a youngster still traumatized by the sudden loss of her parents. She also wrote of her disappointment at having been denied a higher education. But gradually her letters grew happier, reflecting girlish enthusiasm for her job in a Polish factory and her own one-room flat, in whose furnishing and decorating she had taken great pleasure.

Joseph Buloff as Yoshke in O. Dimov's Yoshke the Musician, *Bucharest, 1931.*

The correspondence with our niece gave my sister, Paula, thrice married but childless, the idea of bringing Lenka over to America and adopting her. Joe and I wholeheartedly offered financial support.

But our efforts were frustrated by Lenka's guardian, who wrote that the young woman was a loyal Communist and would never consent to living in capitalist America.

A chance for happiness seemed to open for Lenka when she fell in love with a young Polish workman, Marek, whom she had met at the factory. The relationship lasted several years, but suddenly the young man stopped seeing her and completely disappeared. Lenka's guardian learned in a chance meeting with Marek's brother that Marek had moved to another city and had married someone else.

He told Lenka, who took it hard. First the loss of her parents and then betrayal by her lover were too much for the sensitive young soul to bear. She went home and committed suicide by gas. Thus my brother's line ended in tragedy.

Our huge success in 1931 did not tempt us to stay on in Rumania. Something told us to seek safety in America again, and we made determined efforts to return and settle there on a permanent basis. The U.S. Consul in Bucharest, who had come to see us act and was sympathetic to our problem, finally—following considerable difficulties and delays—secured immigration visas for us. Buloff described it in the following letter:

To Guskin, president of the Hebrew Actors Union.

Bucharest
July 29, 1931

Dear friend, Mr. Guskin:

I have written little to you simply because we have been expecting, any minute now, to be returning to the USA. The American consul in Bucharest with whom we are well acquainted, did not wish to take responsibility for readmitting us on a visitors' permit, since our last extension clearly stated that no new employment contracts or further extension applications would be granted. If the consul were to issue visas to us, he would be violating Washington's ruling. So he slaps us with one hand and strokes with the other.

The consul has approved our immigration status, but since we are not Rumanian but Polish citizens, he referred us to Warsaw for visa numbers, under the visa allotments for Poland for the coming year. The year starts on July 15. The local consul secretary assured us that the consul in Poland will respect the recommendation of the consul in Rumania, and will surely grant the visas. We are therefore told that we will have to wait no more than two or three weeks.

By our count, we should be back in New York by August 20-25 because we plan to leave as soon as we have word from the consul.

We have been a big hit so far. Scheduled for ten performances in Bucharest and then for a tour of the provinces, we have already done seventy performances at this theatre and are scheduled to appear next in an open-air park. Probably we will never go on tour.

The trouble is that we must take in 172 lei before we make one Dollar. But even so, we will have enough when we get to New York to settle our back dues with the union.

Of course, it isn't easy to renounce the success to which we have grown accustomed here. All the same, as soon as we get our visas, we will wire you as to when to expect us.

Respectfully,
Joseph Buloff

Depression

After a brief stop in Berlin for its pulsating theatre scene, we returned to New York and rented a one-bedroom apartment at the southeast corner of Second Avenue and 12th Street—close both to the Cafe Royale, the actors' hangout, and to the Second Avenue theatres. Then we went straight to work, as Buloff related in the following letter:

To Sterenbergf, a Bucharest writer-director.

New York
November 19, 1931

Dear friend Sterenbergf,

Here we are again, blinded by the lights and deafened by the roar of New York.

Perhaps I ought to describe our European triumphs or our sea voyage. But at the gates of New York stands an angel who gives you a snap under the nose as you pass, and instantly you forget where you have come from and where you have been. You arrive naked like the newborn baby that must start life from the beginning. Do not think that this is empty talk!

When we arrived in New York, we were immediately taken by car to the theatre, where the actors were waiting, and we began rehearsing right away.

That first day, we rented an apartment, moved in with furniture, hung up our pictures and had the feeling that we had never been away. The entire Rumanian interlude seemed like a dream, especially since our New York actors, who are usually privy to every trouble in Europe, had apparently heard nothing about our triumphs in Rumania. Vaguely they recall having read in *Literarische Blaetter* something about an interview of Leib Kadison, but where or when they do not know.

We came upon such typical New York snobbery: "Who cares? Rumania? Some country! Some theatre!"

If I had the time, I would tell them a thing or two. But from the start, I got involved in hard work. The Yiddish Theatre has changed little in the time we were away. I am not one of those pessimists who predict that if not tomorrow then the day after tomorrow we will be saying *kaddish* for the Yiddish Theatre. But it is even more tragic as a living corpse.

Every night I look through the peephole in the curtain at the dear grandpas and grandmas seated in upholstered comfort at Second Avenue theatres, and I remember how we used to run around looking for a chair to accommodate cabinet ministers, lest they suffer the discomfort of the hard benches at the Bucharest theatre. And where is that joyful clamor of student fans?

Maurice Schwartz has not been successful on the American stage and is expected soon to return to the Yiddish Theatre. The Ensemble

Theatre (after Schwartz left) suffered a disaster with Leivick's *Golem*. Alexander Granach was hooted off the stage by a wild mob shouting, "We want Michelesko."★ He then joined the Ensemble Theatre, but has since left it. Rubin toured with his vehicle, *The Big Winner* by Sholom Aleichem, got a few hard knocks from local old timers, and was forced to switch to the *Yeshiveh Bocher* by Zolotorefsky. On the whole, then, I have no good news for you. The Yiddish Theatre here is in trouble. It is unpleasant even to talk about it.

Believe me, I prefer to remember our good times in Rumania. The Yiddish Theatre there was lively and colorful; here it is pale and sickly.

Be well! Regards to Sandow and to all good people in Bucharest. And write about what is happending there. What are you doing? Regards from the Kadisons and Luba.

Yours,
B.

To Zarifopel, a leading Rumanian critic.

New York
February 20, 1932

Dear friend,

What a joy to receive a letter from you! It is a wonderful feeling—especially for an actor who is all too conscious of his laurels—to realize that, however long the curtain may have been down behind him, his friends still remember him fondly.

I presume you would like to hear first about Luba and me. Well, there is quite a lot to tell. I wish I were now sitting with you in our usual corner of the *Teatril Now*, having another of our long conversations.

In your letter, you say you are particularly interested in my opinion of the Berlin theatre. Actually, we spent too little time in Berlin for me to form an exhaustive view. But the little we saw was absolutely grand. *Die Schoene Helena* by Offenbach, produced by Reinhart, was flawless as a directorial feat. But I must say the acting did not measure up, and—probably for this reason—we responded to it coolly, despite the magnificent staging.

For good acting, we turned to another theatre, featuring an unimportant play. The scintillating sets, lights and costumes in Max Reinhart's clever presentation did not excite me as much as did a certain actor, Felix Bressart. I have always believed that the actor is the main factor in the theatre.

It may be different on the screen. (I am not too well acquainted with the inner mechanics of the film industry to argue the point.) On the screen, minor talents can be magnified by the amazing tricks of the camera. With the help of highly developed lenses, a flea can be made to act like an elephant. On the stage, the actor is exposed from head to toe, all the time. He walks a tightrope from point to point.

In the theatre, it is not the points that count, but the balancing on the rope. In the movies, the points are the things that count. In films, one walks, one falls; one cries, one laughs. In the theatre, what is important

★ A musical-comedy star.

is how one walks, how one falls, how one begins to cry and then switches from tears to laughter.

Speaking of movies: in Berlin we saw the first sound picture of the great Max Palemberg—what a pitiful sight!—and a Russian film played by kids—*The Road to Life*, which shows considerable merit. It is now opening in New York, and I am sure it will cause a sensation. It contains some of that great Russian pathos and theatricality that is so tremendously effective even through the medium of the camera.

We also attended the premier of *The Last* by the very popular Russian writer Katayev:★ a light satire on current conditions in Russia. It was execrably played, and the poor author, who had come to Berlin from Russia especially to see his play, seemed heartbroken when we met him later.

The theatre world of New York has been severely obscured by the heavy clouds of the depression—this unexpected, inexplicable crisis that swept the country, causing increasing unemployment, a peculiar climate of insecurity, and a nearly chaotic state of affairs. If not remedied in time, this blessed country will know even worse days.

Just a few years ago, there were over eighty theatres on Broadway. Less than half remain open. And with few exceptions, they are not doing well. The poor Yiddish Theatre seems to be fading away.

Under these circumstances, I can hardly tell you anything exciting about me. I am taking it easy, I go to art exhibits and concerts and read good books.

We are all in good health. Luba and her parents send regards. Greetings to your wife and children and to all the good people I had the pleasure of meeting in your home.

Affectionately,
B.

★ Years later, Buloff would play in Katayev's *The Whole World Over* on Broadway.

On to Buenos Aires

One day a young man who had seen and admired Buloff in Chicago came to our tiny Second Avenue apartment. An aspiring producer, he pledged to bring Buloff to the Broadway stage. His was no idle promise, for this young producer was none other than Mike Todd, and he eventually did open the door for Joe to the English-language theatre. But that did not happen until 1937. Meanwhile, we were a pair of Yiddish actors in need of employment in the early years of the depression. Buloff determined that our best opportunity lay in a tour to the Jewish audiences of Argentina, and he wrote the following letter to Mideh, an Argentine-Jewish producer:

New York
January 20, 1932

Dear Mideh,

We agree to all your terms, except for the stipulation that we produce two plays a week. We say no to that. Because it would lead to a sure flop.

You contend that Maurice Schwartz, as big an actor as I am, did three pieces a week. First of all, I am not a Schwartz performer. Secondly, I don't know how he did it. Thirdly, I cannot do it. And fourthly, you don't need it. Because you would lose the bit of money that you might have made with Schwartz if I had to produce three plays a week.

Unless your audiences are so backward that you can bang them over the head at will, your idea does not make sense.

You say that your public comes to see faces and names. Let me tell you that my name means nothing. Buloff is a Gentile name. Lots of Jews can't even pronounce it, and call me Billem. As for my face, I must inform you that I am no matinee idol, and it is doubtful that my face could accomplish very much for you.

So what I promise you is a revolution: instead of having three plays in one week, let us start with one play in three weeks. Believe me, that will save my face, your face and, as a result, your pocketbook.

We consent to the rest of your sixteen conditions. Now you agree to our one condition. And please reply.

Yours,
Buloff

First appearance in Buenos Aires, 1932: Luba Kadison and Joseph Buloff with producer Silberzweig.

February 1932

Dear Mr. Mideh,

  Instead of improving on your first proposal, you made it worse. I don't understand how, after offering us $250 per week, you now propose $800 per month. Nor do I understand the matter of Mme. Friedman.★

  You say that her difficulties with Schwartz were no more than a simple conflict of ambition between two stars. You make me laugh. We are absolutely not interested in traveling thousands of miles to do battle with anyone.

  Therefore, I can think of only one solution. Since, in your words, Mme. Friedman proved to be more successful on the tour than Jacob Ben-Ami, I propose that while Luba and I perform in Buenos Aires, you send Friedman to the provinces.

Here are my terms:

1. The contract shall run two months;
2. We shall be guaranteed $200 per week to be paid out every Sunday night;
3. The ship voyage shall be prepaid (see Point 9);
4. We shall start a week after our arrival;
5. We shall be announced as follows:
  Guest appearances
  by Joseph Buloff
  and Luba Kadison;
6. I shall consult you about casting;
7. Only one play a week;
8. For authors' royalties, 750 pesos per night;
9. A special benefit shall be given after the eighth week, from which we shall receive 70 percent and you, 30 percent (from this we shall deduct what we owe you for round-trip ship tickets);
10. The contract shall take effect the day of our debut;
11. Payment for a full week shall be executed on the first Sunday.

  We have heard rumors that Molly Picon is opening in Buenos Aires at the same time that we are. The press will no doubt allot her lots of space, which will weaken interest in our appearance.

  Her husband, Jacob Kalich, is a master of publicity, and it would therefore be advisable for us to start our performances a week later.

  I am sure you are enough of a theatre man to know how to handle such situations.

Yours,
Buloff

The Argentine venture proved successful, despite an early setback, which Buloff described in a letter to President Guskin of the Hebrew Actors Union:

★ She was Mideh's wife.

Poster announcing production of J. Swerling and E. Robinson's Kibbitzer, *starring Joseph Buloff and Luba Kadison, Buenos Aires, 1932.*

Buenos Aires
1932

Dear Mr. Guskin,

I received your warm letter. You will be interested to hear about our guest appearances in Buenos Aires and our unusual current situation.

At the time we were invited to come to Argentina, you were out of town. Yet you must have meanwhile heard something about the tragicomic circumstances in which we found ourselves. Just before departure, we sublet our apartment, shipped or stored our possessions, and spent $180 on visas, passports and other necessary documents. We were ready to board ship, when one day before the scheduled sailing, we received a telegram: "DO NOT COME!"

You can imagine our shock. We have spent $180 for nothing, and we did not know how to reclaim our property, either from the ship's hold or from the warehouse. We did have round-trip ship tickets, however, and Weintraub and Reilkin (union managers) advised us to ignore the barely intelligible telegram and sail on to Argentina. What could we lose so long as the tickets were valid both ways? Once in Buenos Aires, we would know whether to stay or sail back home. In any event, we will have spent four pleasurable weeks at sea for $180.

So off we went. At the port of Buenos Aires, we were met by the producer, Señor Mideh, who promptly advised us that he was in the middle of a fight with his partner and expected us—as long as we were here—to side with him against this partner.

The partner, a Spaniard, was waiting for us, too. He began shouting at us in Spanish, with voice and gestures and with such force that we thought he was going to tear us to pieces.

After the Spaniard had spoken for five minutes, we asked Mideh, "What did he say?"

Mideh exclaimed: "Let him go to hell! He doesn't know what he is talking about."

I asked Mideh to tell his partner that I did not understand Spanish, but that—since he evidently wished to speak to me personally—we could go to a hotel and, from there, call a member of the press to act as an interpreter.

Mideh's translation of my few words stretched into a five-minute sermon. The Spaniard shot back at him with foam on his lips. I grew impatient and yelled at Mideh: "What, in God's name, is he saying?"

Again Mideh equivocated: "Let him drop dead! You are better off not knowing what he is saying."

Finally, the Spaniard led us into his car and drove to his office—where we were asked to sign a new contract.

"Why?" said I. "I have a contract with Mr. Mideh."

"Mideh, what Mideh? I don't even let him into my office."

When the press heard about our arrival, it firmly and enthusiastically rallied behind us—not like in New York.

The Buenos Aires community is perfect for Yiddish Theatre, and—determined to conquer it—we agreed to all the terms of the Spanish manager.

He owns a theatre in the decaying outskirts of town, at which he insisted that we perform first rather than at a playhouse in the center of Buenos Aires, because of the lower expenses there. Most of the time, he keeps it closed, lest it compete with his two big movie houses.

In that slum theatre, we made our local debut in *Periphery* by Fritz Lang. May we always be so successful! When our Spaniard saw our

As "He" in L. Pirandello's He, She and the Ox.

As Graf Pototsky in A. Kacyzne's Ger Tsedek.

Joseph Buloff in various roles, Argentina, 1930's and 1940's

As the old man in E. O'Neill's Desire Under the Elms.

As Sergei in M. Artsybashev's Jealousy.

production, he tore up the old contract and moved us straight into one of the biggest theatres in the center of the city.

Under our new contract, we are bound to mount a new play every week. Ironically, this Spanish producer has shown himself to be one of the finest persons we have ever encountered in the theatre world. If he asked us to creep on stage on all fours, I would do it, just to please him.

Every two weeks, we present a new play—with sets, extras, music. Our producer wants big spectacles. Therefore, I have put a bed in my dressing room, and I sleep there. And let me tell you, on those hard boards of the dressing room, I dream sweet dreams of adulation and success—better than in a featherbed in New York.

A wonderful eight weeks passed, and the time came to tour the provinces, as stipulated by the contract.

When your wire with Schwartz's offer arrived, we felt that it would be unwise to break off with a friendly Spaniard, to fly back to an envious Jew.

In fact, we are reluctant to tour the Argentine provinces, because it is very tiring. Yet after our success, a number of Argentine producers have come to us with offers to keep us here all year.

Four theatres have merged, and there is a demand for actors—as a result of which the the actors got together and formed a union. They have not picked a leader as yet, because everyone is a leader. Instead of helping each other, they envy and hinder each other. The owners of the theatre where Michelesko and Picon are appearing want us to play for them as soon as their guest stars leave. Competing though they are with our Spanish producer, they are urging him to sell them our contract. As he realizes that we are in great demand, he extended our run and set a high price for our contract. If they don't accept it, he will send us off to the provinces. He is negotiating, and we are waiting.

Dear friend, I know you have enough headaches of your own. So I will end my letter.

Yours,
Joseph Bulof and Luba Kadison

Nowhere in the Western Hemisphere did we find a better audience for the repertoire of the original Vilna Troupe than in Buenos Aires. Apart from the play mentioned in Buloff's letters, we successfully produced on our first tour *The Singer of His Sorrow* and *The Dybbuk*.

In the 1930's, Argentina had a thriving Jewish community. Because immigration there had continued beyond the peak, pre-quota years of the United States, Buenos Aires had a young Yiddish-speaking population, with many immigrant families passing the language down to their native-born children. These Yiddish speakers were proud that their language rang on the stage, and they eagerly observed and absorbed its dramatic classics.

Crowds besieged our theatre, and tickets sold briskly. Traffic had to be diverted from the streets around the theatre because of the throngs. The press placed us on a pedestal. Jewish and Argentine critics alike, journalists and theatre people, all acclaimed and enjoyed our performances.

We appeared on the guest-star system, with Joe and me in the leading roles, and local actors in the supporting parts. This enabled us to discover and make friends

Poster announcing a special evening devoted to selections performed by Luba Kadison, Buenos Aires, 1939.

with young local talent—Bertha Singerman (a great Spanish-language recital artist), Paulina Singerman, Leo Halpern and his wife, Esther.

Jacobo Muchnik, a prominent Jewish publisher of Spanish books and periodicals, became our closest lifelong friend. It all began one evening, when he and his wife, Elisa, had taken a stroll in midtown, passing our theatre, and, attracted by the posters for *Singer of His Sorrow*, caught the second act. Entranced by our performances, they came backstage, introduced themselves and invited us to their home. Performance after performance, Muchnik sat in the front row and snapped hundreds of photos of us. Today, years and years later, having left Buenos Aires and established himself in Barcelona, he still corresponds with me.

Between the 1930's and 1960's, we returned many times to Buenos Aires. With the seasons there reversed, we could play an entire winter in New York, then sail (later, fly) to Argentina in June and do a second winter season there.

The plays we presented in subsequent tours to Buenos Aires, Rio de Janeiro, Montevideo, and other South American cities included The *Kibbitzer*, *Anna Karenina*, *Ger Tsedek*, *Gaslight*, *The Diary of Anne Frank*, *Fishke*, *Death of a Salesman*, *Chains*, *Desire Under the Elms*, and *The 60,000 Heroes*.

In *Anna Karenina*, I played the title role. Shortly before, Garbo had been cast in the movie version as the tragic Russian heroine, which set high standards to aim for. As I struggled with the part in rehearsals, I overheard a local actor saying "She'll never bring it off." Thereupon I resolutely summoned up all my years of experience with the Vilner, all my training with past masters like Mme. Visotska, Leib Kadison, David Herman and Joseph Buloff, and in the end earned a gratifying ovation. Anna Karenina has remained my favorite role. The play also proved to be our greatest financial success.

Buloff successfully captured the atmosphere in the Jewish theatre in New York and Buenos Aires in the following letters:

To Leivick, poet, playwright, author of *The Golem* and *Chains*.

Buenos Aires
1934

Dear friend Leivick,

I guess you are justifiably angry at me for not writing. But you will surely forgive me when I tell you that in the last eight weeks I have presented nine plays here.

Under such circumstances, one not only neglects writing to a friend but also goes completely crazy.

Actually, this letter is a rewrite of the one I drafted a week ago, before I staged your *Chains*.★ I was about to mail the original letter when I read in the Yiddish papers the unhappy news about your health problem. You had also reportedly left New York.

I wanted to mail you your royalties; but how? The Argentine peso has plunged, and the government has forbidden the transfer of money outside of the country.

★ A play about political prisoners before the Russian Revolution.

*Luba Kadison in various roles, Argentina, 1930's and 1940's: (top) as
Sonya in F. Dostoyevsky's* Crime and Punishment; *(bottom) as The
Witch in* A Chekhov Sketchbook.

Luba Kadison in various roles, Argentina, 1930's and 1940's (continued): (top) as Anna Karenina in L. Tolstoi's Anna Karenina, *with Joseph Buloff as Karenin; (bottom) as Bruriah in D. Pinsky's* Bruriah.

I appealed to the local Literary Society for help in sending you the money I had collected for you. But they cannot help. Then I figured that in a few weeks I would no doubt be back in New York and could personally deliver the cash to you. That would avoid lots of complications and bother.

Under the contract that I was forced to sign upon arrival, a play cannot be performed for more than one week. Yet I am more than certain that *Chains* could have run three weeks. The Spanish producer might have let it run longer, despite the contract. Strangely, however, certain scenes elicited applause from part of the audience and whistling from the other part. The public was clearly divided into antagonistic camps, and someone alerted the producer that he might become involved with the police. As a result, *Chains* aroused overwhelming interest, which a smart producer would have exploited. But our producer doesn't understand why your audiences should be either pro or con; he fails to see what the controversy is all about.

We will repeat *Chains* in another theatre with another producer. Meanwhile, the present producer, who is a good sort, has promised to forward your royalties. He owns several movie houses here and has ties with the United States.

The main thing is that you get well.

> Yours
> Buloff

To Benjamin Ressler, author of *The 60,000 Heroes*.

> Buenos Aires
> September 11, 1934

Dear Ressler,

Ten days ago I wrote you a letter, and now I am writing another, because—you will be glad to hear—we are preparing to present *The 60,000 Heroes*.

As I said in my previous letter, we were about to conclude our guest-appearance season here and return to New York. Our luggage was packed, and on the morrow we were supposed to board ship. But that evening at the farewell party thrown for us by our friend, the publisher Jacobo Muchnik, in a private home, I read *The 60,000 Heroes* to the guests, and they loved it so much that they decided not to let us leave and insisted that we premiere the play right here in Buenos Aires. We unpacked and went straight to work.

Everything is being done to promote it. The Yiddish press (*Der Yiddish Zeitung* and *Die Presse*), as well as the Spanish newspapers, which gave us support during our guest appearances, is helping with a lot of publicity now.

Much depends, of course, on the audiences, among whom we count a great many admirers. If the public likes the play, all will be well.

Now about royalties: I got 100 pesos for you immediately, with the understanding that if the play catches on, you shall receive another 100. But there is still the problem of forwarding you the money, for after the peso so dramaticlly tumbled lately—the government has prohibited money transfers outside the country. It was difficult enough to obtain permission to send you the first 100 pesos through a bank.

Joseph Buloff as a crusader in B. Ressler's 60,000 Heroes, *Buenos Aires, 1934.*

If at all possible, have the New York Jewish newspapers run a notice about the presentation of *The 60,000 Heroes* in Buenos Aires. It will come in handy if we ever present the drama in New York.

Yours,
Buloff

To Leo and Esther Halpern, Buenos Aires actors.

New York
July 24, 1933

Dear friends Leo and Esther,

Finally we got a letter from you. We thought you had forgotten all about us.

At present, we are at Sea Gate—a separate community in Brooklyn near the ocean, consisting of 100 small homes surrounded by a fence. It is alleged to have once been populated mainly by Germans who had placed a policeman at the gate to prevent anyone but residents from entering. The policeman is still here, but now most of the residents are Jews.

We will spend the whole summer here. On Sundays we go to New York City to appear on the radio ("The Forward Hour," WEVD).

I am very interested in the goings on in your theatre world, because we are not through with Argentina yet. If not this year, then next we will perform together again.

You may have read about us in the press, and about the new enterprise of the producer Sachs: quite a sensation. Sachs is the last of the old-time Jewish producers who once amassed a fortune from the *shund* theatre. But then he turned his back on cheap melodrama, having either come to his senses or lost his mind, and for substantial fees he engaged Peretz Hirschbein, David Pinsky, Osip Dimov, and Benjamin Ressler. He hung up huge portraits of these playwrights in his lobby, invited all the theatre critics to a fine dinner, and announced that he was completely changing the style and content of his theatre. Naturally, this caused a sensation, and into this uproar we walked on our return from South America.

This summer we were supposed to travel to Poland, to play in *The 60,000 Heroes*—I have improved the script—but Hitler has put all such plans on hold. With the mounting panic among the Jews there, no talk of theatre or of raising money for plays is possible.

We have been strongly advised not to go to Europe because war might break out. Whether or not that is absurd, we are heeding the warning and are sticking to radio work.

At one point, Sachs suddenly came to us with a surprise offer. After all the excitement about the writers he had engaged Aaron Lebedov—rumored to be the wealthiest Jewish performer, and a financial backer of Sachs's new enterprise.

I wondered what I could do in collaboration with Lebedov. He is a charming entertainer, a true son of the Jewish people, and in his genre he is the very best. With his thrown-back shoulders and roguish eyes, a straw hat down over his brow, a stylish cane in hand plus his folksy Litvak

Salón "Kadima" Moisés Ville

GRAN ESPECTACULO
por los eminentes artistas
José Buloff - Liuba Kadison
secundados por el actor HERMAN LASTER

Domingo 29
a las 21.45 horas
Unica Función

נאר איין פֿאָרשטעלונג

אין סאלאָן "קאַדימה"

יוסף בולאָוו-ליובאַ קאַדימאָן

צוזאַמען מיט דעם באַקאַנטן שוישפּילער הערמאַן לאַסטער

זונטיק דעם 29-טן דעצעמבער 1935

פּראָגראַם:

(1) דער נסיון - פֿון דוד פּינסקי

(2) די מכשפֿה - (קאָמעדיע) - פֿון א. טשעכאָוו

(3) סצענעס פֿון גרינע פֿעלדער פֿון פּרץ הירשביין

צום סוף קאָנצערט אָפּטיילונג

גערענקט

איינמאָל אין משך פֿון יאָרן קענט איר דא באַוואונדערן אזעלכע קינסטלער.
נוצט אויס די געלעגנהייט!

Precios de las localidades: **Platea: filas 1 al 5 $ 2.—; 6 al 14 $ 1.50; restantes $ 1.—
Palcos bajos $ 8.— - Palcos altos $ 5.— - Tertulia $ 0.80**

בילעטן צו באַקומען בא אברהם יעדלין.

דרוק "שיינין און מולער" מאָזעסוויל

Broadside announcing performance by Joseph Buloff and Luba Kadison, Moisésville, Argentina, 1935.

accent, he projects the true image and soul of the Jewish musical entertainer. The best lover on the Yiddish stage, but this young lover is unfortunately 59 years old. It is hard for him to do a dance, and his voice is a bit hoarse and ragged. Offstage he is as charming as he is on stage. But the question remained, how do we two fit? What could we play together in the theatre?

We let Sachs's proposal hang in the air for eight whole weeks. Meanwhile, he hired Samuel Goldenberg and made an offer to Jacob Ben-Ami and Satz. Celia Adler is also in his company. And Dinah Abramovich, too.

He engaged two of the best young actors, Zvi Scooler and Michel Rosenberg, as well. And finally Luba and I signed, too. It will be interesting to see what comes of it. Peretz Hirschbein is writing his first musical play, which will naturally be the most important factor.

By the time you receive this letter, Schwartz will be producing *Yoshe Kalb*★ in Buenos Aires. It was a big hit in New York, and he made lots of money.

We are in frequent correspondence with our friend Jacobo Muchnik. He insists that we come back to Argentina soon.

There is little to report on the English-language theatre. It seems to me that the movies and radio are increasingly impairing the rich American theatre. A few years ago, there were 80 working theatres on Broadway—40 to 50 in the summer season. Now only a fraction remains. Rockefeller has built two enormous movie palaces—the largest in the world. Together they accommodate 10,000 viewers per performance and 50,000 per day. Go compete with that!

Yours,
B.

**Theatro
Casino Antarctica**

Rua Anhangabaú — Tel. 4-7703

Sexta-Feira, dia 24 de Fevereiro
as 9 horas
Primeiro Espetaculo dos Grandes Artistas

**Josef Buloff
e
Luba Kadison**

פרײַטאָג, דעם 24-טן פעברואר 9 אוונט
ערשטע פארשטעלונג פון די וועלט בארימטע קינסטלער

יוסף בולאוו

און

ליובא קאדיסאן

מיטן אנטייל פון די באליבטע ארטיסטן

אסתר פערעלמאן און יצחק דײַטש

ווערט אויפגעפירט צום ערשטן מאל אין סאן פאולא
דאָס גרויסע קונסט-שטיק אין דרײַ אקטן פון
פרץ הירשביין

די גרינע פעלדער

עס נעמט אנטייל די גאנצע אסטאאירינדע טרופע
בילעטן פרײַזן פון 3$500 ביז 11$500 (מיט סעלאס)
צו באקומען אין באר ושאקאב, ושאוע פאולינא 150 און
פון דאנערשטיק אין קאסע פון טעאטער קאסינא

Broadside announcing production of P. Hirschbein's
Green Fields, *starring Joseph Buloff and Luba
Kadison, São Paulo, 1939.*

★ By I.J. Singer.

Mordecai Mazo

Encouraged by the Buenos Aires Yiddish Theatre's warm reception, Buloff began to dream again of reviving the Vilna Troupe, and, in a letter to its original manager, Mordecai Mazo, outlines an ambitious plan.

Buenos Aires
1932

Dear Mazo,

It has been several weeks since I received your communication, and I must apologize for my delay in replying. But you do understand the complex nature of a Yiddish actor's job if he is also involved in artistic projects. So much time and energy are expended in wheeling and dealing with halfwits or madmen who call themselves producers. So much effort must be invested in serious plays! And the greatest of successes brings but small rewards. The casts are so large that even packed houses can hardly sustain the expenses of long tours.

Not many producers are interested in artistic Yiddish productions. Therefore, we tend to accept the first reasonable proposal, even if it comes from some fly-by-night producer who squeezes us like a lemon once he has us in hand.

Buenos Aires, I must tell you, is the best place for Yiddish Theatre today. If only you were here, we could do good work together. I would be happy if that could happen.

However, from your letter I understand that we probably will have to come to you in Europe. If you cannot find a place in Warsaw, it might be a good idea to meet in Paris. We have an offer to perform in France and would like to collaborate with you. But you know how hard it is to move with a whole troupe these days. Most countries have closed their borders and do not admit aliens, especially Jews. Then there are the unions, who are not pleased if a whole troupe appears in their land.

The only practical formula, in my opinion, is guest appearances. To keep alive the tradition of the Vilna Troupe, I have hatched a wild idea. Let us establish in the few Jewish communities where art theatre is still possible a nucleus of Vilner. What I mean is, let us find the scattered Vilna actors and bring them together in these Jewish centers.

The directors and principal actors would travel from one group to the other, to stage the same plays. Box office receipts and subsidies would be shared. It is either a great idea or a crazy plan. But what other way could you devise for the Vilna Troupe to travel? In my view, no other system is possible.

Guest appearances remain the only means, and I would like to be associated with you in such an enterprise. So I would like to hear from you before we go further.

Luba also greets you and our dear Orleska.

Yours,
Buloff

Nothing came out of this scheme. Mazo continued to manage the Vilna Troupe in Warsaw until World War II. Our communications with him ceased with the invasion of Poland in 1939, with only few scattered, indirect reports filtering through. A horrifying rumor reached us—and is still haunting me—that Mazo lost his mind under Nazi persecution and ran about the Warsaw Ghetto raving mad.

Age and starvation might have unhinged his mind and he might have imagined that he was back in the Vilna of World War I, organizing his Troupe with the tacit approval of German conquerors who still retained a shred of humanity.

Recently, some light was shed for me on the fate of the Vilna Troupe veterans by two Holocaust survivors, the publisher Donat and his wife. Miriam Orleska, Mazo's life companion—who had had the misfortune of returning from Russia to Warsaw as the war broke out—had stayed with them outside the Ghetto, and then was forced to move into the Ghetto. From there she had been taken to the *Umschlagsplatz* (assembly place) for transportation to a death camp, where she perished. Mazo apparently had been with her to the very end.

With him also perished the Vilna Troupe. Had the horror of the Holocaust not occurred, the Troupe might have survived to this day. With a keen eye for new acting, directorial and literary talent, with his business acumen, with his devotion to Yiddish, Mazo might have kept the company alive and active; and eventually he might have passed it on to a younger generation. A Yiddish-speaking population in Eastern Europe could have sustained it.

Mordecai Mazo

Alas, this was not to be! The same evil force that destroyed the Jews of Europe destroyed our theatre, too. All that remains of the Vilna Troupe is a memory of *The Dybbuk*, *The Singer of His Sorrow* and more than 150 other productions.

Joseph Buloff recognized Mazo's contribution to the Vilna Troupe. He once wrote in a letter:

"Mazo was the one who lasted through all the splits, all the reformations, all the glorious traditions of the original Vilna Troupe."

Second Avenue

Upon our return from Argentina, we signed with the producer Sachs to do *A Meisseh Fun Amol* (*A Tale of Long Ago*), by Peretz Hirschbein—with music by Lazar Weiner and an all-star cast. It did not score with the public, however, because it was too literary for the commercial stage.

This setback caused Sachs to revert to his previous fare of popular music shows. To my surprise, he asked me to stay on, offering me the leading part as a gypsy maiden in *Katarintchek* (*The Organ Grinder*), a musical, with the operetta star Julius Nathanson. I hesitated, for I had never done popular musicals, but agreed at least to read the part. As I saw its potential, I ultimately accepted it, especially since it included the prestige of a solo.

But upon hearing the song—a hearts and flowers tune—I realized that it contributed nothing either to an understanding of the character or to the furthering of the plot. I outlined my own concept to the composer, Alexander Olshanetsky, and his lyricist, Chaim Tauber: The song of the gypsy, whom I was to portray, had to arise from, and tie in with, my fortune-telling action on stage. I would read in the cards my own fortune, painfully foresee my lover's imminent betrayal and raise my voice in a mournful lament—singing about the force of my love and the grief in my heart even as I wished my faithless lover all happiness.

Olshanetsky and Tauber gratefully made my idea their own, producing "Ich Hub Dich Tsufil Lieb," which I interpreted in the style of high drama and turned into a hit. Translated as "I Love You Much Too Much," it became a popular American song.

I sang it on many occasions, becoming identified with it, although I never received a cent in royalties for it. *Katarintchek* proved to be so popular that we took it on tour to major U.S. cities and Canada. The following season, Sachs offered to star me with Ludwig Satz and Michel Michelesko in another musical.

At that point, however, I had the choice of accompanying Joe for a second time to Argentina and doing our classical Yiddish repertory there. I never hesitated. It was on to Buenos Aires.

That second season in South America brought me accolades for my portrayal of Anna Karenina and the frightened heroine of *Gaslight*—two of my favorite roles. Upon our return to the States, I rejoined Maurice Schwartz's company and on and off played for seven years with the Yiddish Art Theatre.

With Schwartz I toured North America, appearing in Montreal, Toronto, Chicago, Boston and Philadelphia. Our main production was the dramatization of *The Brothers Ashkenazi* by I.J. Singer, in which I played Dinah, the unhappy wife of the elder brother, Meyer, portrayed by Schwartz. The play proved so successful that in 1938 Schwartz took it, with me, to Paris and London. There we also

Broadside listing the members of the Second Ave. Theatre Company, New York, 1933-34 season.

presented *Yoshe Kalb*. The friendship and warmth of my fellow performers and of the stage manager, Katz, helped me cope with Joe's absence: I missed him terribly.

Europe was already tense and apprehensive, sensing the inevitability of war. But we were immersed in our work, and the Jewish audiences took some comfort in the sound of Yiddish.

In Paris, at a banquet honoring the cast, I found myself seated next to Marc Chagall, already recognized but not yet on a worldwide scale. He spoke to me in Russian, yet greatly enjoyed my recitation of Yiddish poetry. On Schwartz's insistence I recited several poems by our old friend from Rumania, Itzhak Manger, whom I and other consider the greatest modern Yiddish poet.

The next day—on Chagall's invitation—Schwartz, his wife and I visited the artist's studio, where my producer requested that I bargain for him on purchasing a painting because my fluent Russian and the artist's favorable disposition toward me might reduce the price.

Chagall stated that all financial matters were handled by his wife, Bella; but as I began negotiating with Bella, I observed that Chagall—even as he was standing behind me—was signalling numbers to his wife with his fingers. I did succeed in getting one painting reduced to a reasonable price, but Schwartz did not buy it. As for myself, I settled for an autographed photo of the master. Looking back on that afternoon, I realize that if Schwartz and I had then acquired a few Chagalls, we would have realized more money in one hour than two lifetimes in the theatre had afforded us.

Another Chagall anecdote: During the war, the painter found refuge in New York, where we renewed our acquaintance. By that time his works had grown too expensive for me even to dream of acquiring one. What I had for him was a business proposal. Buloff and I were thinking of reviving our Yiddish musical revue, *The Rainbow*, in an English translation, and I proposed to Chagall that he design the sets so that we could stage it in his own unique style—as an evocation of his hometown, Vitebsk. Surely, that would make the production ideal for Broadway.

In his luxurious hotel suite, Marc Chagall, conscious of his towering reputation, walked to the window, looked out for a while, and then slowly said in Yiddish: "Well, if Leonard Bernstein did the music and Jerome Robbins handled the choreography, I might think about it." We never did bring *The Rainbow* to Broadway.

Touring with Schwartz did not consist exclusively of banquets and meetings with celebrities like Chagall. I can recall times on our American tour when the box office returns were disappointingly low, and Schwartz would summon the entire company, turn out his pockets, and declare: "I have no money to pay your salaries. So sue me!" With luck, we had enough money to get to the next town, hoping that there business would pick up so that our grand producer could pay his actors.

I discovered that Schwartz had a wry sense of humor. Once, for instance, the actor Anatole Winogradof suffered a memory lapse in the middle of his performance as the rabbi in *Shylock's Daughter*, and audibly exploded in English: "God damn it, I forgot my lines." He presently recovered after someone threw him a cue, finished his performance and, fearing Schwartz,

DAVIDSON THEATRE
Third and Wisconsin Avenues

FOR ONLY ONE PERFORMANCE!
Sunday Evening, April 12th, 1936

JOSEPH BULOFF IN "FISHKE DER KRUMER"

Only One Performance in Milwaukee
Sunday Evening, Apr. 12

Luba Kadison

The Jewish Drama Society
OF CHICAGO

Presents

The Celebrated Yiddish Stage Artists
Joseph Buloff
and
Luba Kadison
IN THE UNIQUE COMEDY

"FISHKE DER KRUMER"

By Mendele Mocher Sforim

with an Ensemble of 50 Selected Assisting Artists.

Entire Stage Settings and Sceneries brought to Davidson Theatre from Chicago
special for this Performance.

Tickets on Sale now at the Box Office of Davidson Theatre.

בלױז 1 פֿאָרשטעלונג
אין מילװאָקי

DAVIDSON THEATRE
Third and Wisconsin Avenues

בלױז 1 פֿאָרשטעלונג
אין מילװאָקי

די בארימטע אידישע קינסטלער פֿון ניו יאָרק

זונטיק אװנט
12 טן אפֿריל

יוסף בולאָװ און ליובא קאַדיסאָן

זונטיק אװנט
12 טן אפֿריל

צוזאַמען מיט דער

שיקאַגער דראמאטישער געזעלשאפֿט

אין דער גרױסער עלפֿאלנגרײכער אױפֿפֿירונג פֿון

פֿישקע דער קרומער

קאָמעדיע פֿון דעם גרױסן אידישן שריפֿטשטעלער מענדעלע מוכר ספֿרים

מוזיק — געזאַנג — מאַסן סצענ
ספּעציעלע דעקאָראַציעס געבראַכט
קײן מילװאָקי.

הומאָר — סאַטירע — געלעכטער

אַנפֿאַנג 8:30 פּונקט.

אַנסאַמבל פֿון העכער
50 שױשפּילער

העכער צען טױזענט מענשען האָבן מיט באַגײַ־
סטערונג באַגריסט די קינסטלער אין דער אױפֿ־
פֿירונג פֿון "פֿישקע דער קרומער" אין שיקאַגע

פּרײַזן פֿון טיקעטס 55 ס., 83 ס. און $1.10
שױן צו באַקומען אין באָקס אָפֿיס פֿון
דײװידסאָן טעאטער.

Broadside announcing production of Mendele Mokher Sefarim's Fishke the Lame, *starring Joseph Buloff and Luba Kadison, Milwaukee, 1936.*

rushed out of the theatre. The next day he found an envelope on his dressing table. Expecting a pink slip, he opened it and read:

If you have to curse on stage, why not in Yiddish?

Yours,
Schwartz

It was to Schwartz's credit that he recognized talent and was willing to import star performers from Europe. When an actor eventually achieved critical acclaim, however, the producer betrayed a flaw in his character: Jealousy. In the 1939 production of *Three Cities*, by Sholem Asch (an elaborate Broadway production with sets by Sam Leve), veteran actor Pavel Baratov appeared in the first act as Old Mirkin, a successful Russian-Jewish attorney in Petrograd, with me as his spoiled daughter-in-law, Nina.

Schwartz portrayed the patriarch of a working-class family who comes on stage only in the second act, set in Warsaw. Both Baratov and Schwartz were perfectly suited for their roles. Yet shortly after the opening, Schwartz called Baratov into his office and asserted: "My public does not wish to wait for the second act to see me. We are switching roles." Whereupon Baratov, deeply offended, left the company.

Another annoying display by Schwartz was his ongoing direction of other players on stage, even while he himself was acting. "Talk louder" or "Talk softer," he would coach others in audible tones during actual performances—enough to shake the confidence of any actor.

Perhaps from respect for my Vilna Troupe background, Schwartz never tried that trick on me. My only open

Luba Kadison as Nina and Maurice Schwartz as the old Mirkin in the Yiddish Art Theatre production of Sholem Asch's Three Cities, *New York, 1940.*

disagreement with him came during the run of *Who Is Who* by Leivick. Schwartz had given the coveted leading female role to his niece—a pretty girl of limited experience. But after three performances her voice gave out, and he called on me to fill the part the next night.

I saw no reason to risk my reputation by stepping unrehearsed into a leading part, and I refused. Svi Scooler, the union representative, sided with Schwartz, but he took me all the same to see Guskin, president of the Hebrew Actors Union, for a final ruling. Although Guskin similarly interpreted the contract as mandating compliance by me, he gave me a broad hint that, in view of the short notice, I could play the part script-in-hand. That seemed to me so unprofessional that I instead chose to stay up all night memorizing the part. In the end, I scored a hit in *Who Is Who*, and kept the part for the remainder of the season.

Later, I toured Boston, Chicago, Philadelphia, Toronto, and other Canadian and American cities with Jacob Ben-Ami and Bertha Gersten. We did *Awake and Sing*, by Odets, and Ibsen's *Ghosts* in Yiddish. There were still audiences for serious Yiddish Theatre.

Luba Kadison as Nina and Jacob Ben-Ami as the young Mirkin in the Yiddish Art Theatre production of Sholem Asch's Three Cities, *New York, 1940.*

Barbara

The year 1941 ushered in significant changes: Buloff secured a part in a long-running Broadway play, succeeding Morris Carnovsky in the role of the eccentric Greek landlord in *My Sister Eileen*. At last, we had an adequate income enabling us to move into a large apartment off Central Park West. Even more important, I took a leave from Schwartz's theatre, because I was expecting a child.

One evening while Buloff was performing in *My Sister Eileen* and I was alone at home reading the script of *Jacobowski and the Colonel* to see if it offered possibilities for him, I felt incipient labor pains and called my obstetrician, who ordered me immediately to Women's Hospital. I was lucky to spot a cab in blacked-out New York, and rushed to the hospital, instantly to be sedated into a state of twilight sleep. When I emerged into full wakefulness, a nurse placed a beautiful baby girl in my arms, and proud Papa Joe arrived immediately after the show, to see what his wife had produced that night.

The miracle was named Barbara. For almost three years I stayed away from the theatre, to give my little daughter a good start in life.

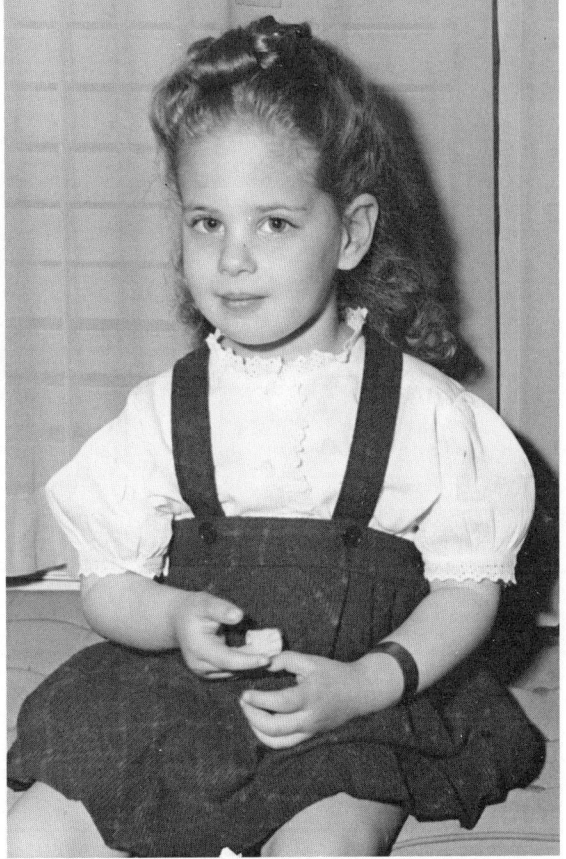

Barbara Buloff at age four.

Barbara Buloff and Joseph Buloff, 1982.

Luba Kadison as Tsinele in P. Hirschbein's Green Fields, *Buenos Aires, 1944.*

When Barbara was about four years old, I took her to see her father in one of his best-remembered roles—the Persian peddler, Ali Hakim, in *Oklahoma!*. In Act Two, when a hulking cowboy struck and knocked Ali Hakim to the floor, a straining voice was heard from the mezzanine: "Don't you hit my daddy!"

By the time Barbara was enrolled in nursery school, I had resumed my career, returning to musical comedy with my appearance in *They All Want To Get Married* (produced by Yehuda Bleich, with Aaron Lebedov, Lucy and Misha Gehrman, and Dinah and Irving Grossman in the cast). During my next two seasons of operettas, I played for Irving Jacobson and Irving Grossman, producers of the Second Avenue Theatre.

Barbara used to watch my performances from the wings. Later, she would join us on our tours of Israel and see her father in some of his most memorable Yiddish roles. Following our example, she took parts in school and camp productions, and later as an undergraduate at Boston University. Joe and I watched her perform and judged her talented. But she changed her direction after college, earned a Master's Degree in social work at Yeshiva University, and is now a successful psychotherapist.

For several years, I accompanied Buloff to South America in the off season. It was gratifying to get back to serious drama and to the receptive audiences of Buenos Aires. During one of the tours, a telegram alerted me that Barbara, whom we had sent to a children's summer camp, was quite ill. Instantly, I flew back to the States, to find my child fully recovered.

In 1949, Buloff obtained from Arthur Miller (through the mediation of Harold Clurman) the release of *Death of a Salesman* for a Yiddish adaptation and its presentation in Buenos Aires. In this form, it scored as well at the box office as it did artistically. But unfortunately, the Peronist government barred any transfer of the proceeds from Argentina.

When Miller demanded his royalties, Buloff proposed to repeat the Yiddish presentation of *Salesman* in New York in order to pay him with the New York returns. As a practical businessman as well as a great playwright, Miller saw the logic of Buloff's idea, and granted permission.

With Buloff in the twin role of director and main protagonist, the play was presented, as a limited engagement, at the Parkway Theatre in Brooklyn. At the insistence of the producers, Goldman and Jacob Jacobson, I played the part of the long-suffering wife, Linda.

Despite doubts as to whether Brooklyn audiences would respond to such a harrowing drama, we realized in the end that the public—which we had underestimated—saw their own lives mirrored in the play and were deeply moved.

Arthur Miller came to our performance and liked it. And in his review in *Commentary* magazine in February 1951, George Ross wrote: "What one feels most strikingly is that the Yiddish play really is the original, and the Broadway production was merely Arthur Miller's translation into English."

Ross praised my Linda for "force, feeling and style," and Buloff's portrayal of Willy Loman as being "in the line of good Jewish realism, akin to French, Italian and Russian styles."

The play was a financial success; Miller got his royalties.

In the long run, episodes such as my sudden, anxious flight from Argentina on learning that Barbara had taken ill, underscoring as they did my primary duty as a mother, caused me, after *Death of a Salesman*, to curtail my appearances as an actress.

Buenos Aires, July 25th., 1949.

Miss Ruth Gordon,
M.C.A. Management,
444 Madison Avenue,
NEW YORK, 22.

Dear Miss Ruth Gordon:

Having played "THE DEATH OF A SALESMAN" in Buenos Aires for seven weeks, I am now writing to you to give a detailed report on the extraordinary success the play has had in this city.

I have not addressed you before as I have had little or np time available, and I understood that Mr. Lawrence Smith, who takes care of your interests in the show here, kept you supplied with general information and write-ups from the newspapers.

However, as the show will be closing in a week, I consider it is a good opportunity to send you all the information that may be of interest to you.

Although the Yiddish speaking community in Buenos Aires is relatively small (abouth 15,000 theatre-goers), the warmth, and particularly the fact of being able to put up a show with very adequate sets and lighting equipment, which are supplied by the community, lures the Yiddish speaking actors to come down for a short while to play for this community in repertory plays, of which each play usually runs from two to three weeks at the most.

It is a very great satisfaction indeed to be able to inform that "THE DEATH OF A SALESMAN" has broken all records, having a run of seven weeks, which means that each member of the community saw it at least twice.

In addition to this, "THE DEATH OF A SALESMAN" created such an interest among the Spanish speaking actors and writers, that I found it necessary to give two special performances for them.

The production, and my performance in the part of the salesman, and the unusual praise in the newspapers, made them realize the possibilities of the play in the Spanish version, and has produced considerable excitment, and I understand several people have applied for the rights of the Spanish version.

On the other hand, one of the most outstanding local actors and movie stars, Pedro López Lagar, has offered to play it in Spanish under my direction, and has told me he will be contacting you through his agent in order to get the rights of the play. Having a direct knowledge, through my personal contacts, of the Argentine theatre world, I would advise you to give preference to his offer, since I consider him the most suitable actor for the part of the salesman.

There is also another important matter which I wish to submit for your consideration. I have received an offer to play "THE DEATH OF A SALESMAN" in the United States. This, of course is entirely dependant on Mr. Muller's authorization, and as

cont.

-2-

he was so kind in allowing me to play the Yiddish version in Buenos Aires, I took the liberty of writing to him directly, explaining the point. As I have received no anser yet, I suppose my letter, which was sent to his address in London, got there to late, so I considered convenient to write to you, as his agent, in order to get his permission.

At the same time, I would appreciate you consider my application for the rights of the Yiddish version in the United States, and I am certain you will give preference to my application, for as you surely know, I have been the first to produce this play in the Yiddish version, and furthermore, I have done the translation from the English version to Yiddish.

These two facts, apart from all my other personal efforts, which have resulted in the Yiddish version being such a "hit", entitle me, I am sure, to be considered before any other offers you may have received. I also wish to inform that I amdready to meet your conditions and requirements on the same level as any other aplicant for the rights of the play in the Yiddish version.

Letter from Joseph Buloff reporting on production of A. Miller's Death of a Salesman *in Buenos Aires, 1949.*

As I told Mr. Muller in my letter, I am sure that had
you seen the Yiddish version, and my interpretation of the
part of the salesman, your would not hesitate in granting me
the permission and the rights for the play. Furthermore, I do
not think the Yiddish version could represent any competition
to the English version, and on the contrary, in my opinion,
the Yiddish version would create quite an interest among the
Yiddish speaking public to see the play in both versions.

Hoping to hear from you at your earliest convenience,
I remain,

Yours respectfully,

Mr. Joseph Buloff,
c/o. Hotel Lyon,
Río Bamba 251,
BUENOS AIRES. (Argentina)

But there was still much that I could do to help Buloff with his career. In 1952, we adapted and translated from Russian into English three Chekhov tales—"The Witch," "The Vagabond" and "In the Music Shop"—which were presented at the Off-Broadway Gramercy Theater under the collective title *The Chekhov Sketchbook*. Joe was sensational as the protagonist in three vastly disparate one-act plays. The critic Brooks Atkinson of the New York Times, and the actor Luther Adler, among many others, climbed up two flights to Buloff's dressing room to congratulate him.

Another English translation that I undertook, together with playwright Sylvia Regan, was that of Buloff's adaptation of Leivick's *Golem*. This script served as the basic libretto for the grand opera, *The Golem*, which was premiered by the New York City Opera Company under the baton of Julius Rudel with music by Abe Ellstein. It failed to garner critical approval, however, and did not remain in the repertory.

I also reworked and rendered into Yiddish *The Diary of Anne Frank*, which Buloff staged with stunning success in Israel; *Inherit the Wind*, which was presented in Buenos Aires with the star performer of the Habimah, Shimon Finkel, in the main role; *Rashomon*; and Durenmatt's *The Visit*.

In the 1960's I served as assistant director to Buloff when he revived *The Brothers Ashkenazi* and *The Singer of His Sorrow* for the Folksbiene in New York. I also often accompanied him on tours of South America and Israel.

Teatro Soleil

CORRIENTES 3150   T. A. (79) 2687

DIRECCION: Stramer, Peltz, Feldbaum, Narepkin

El insigne actor
Joseph BULOFF
en

La Muerte de un Vendedor

Drama de la vida real original de
ARTHUR MILLER
En 2 actos
Puesta en escena por Joseph Buloff

REPARTO

Willy Loman .... Joseph Buloff
Lisa (su esposa) .... Clara Stramer
Benny (su hijo mayor) .... José Maurer
Harry (su hijo menor) .... Aaron Alexandroff
Charlie (su amigo) .... Sascha Rosental
Bernardo (hijo de Charlie) ...... Julio Novominsky
Sem (hermano de Willy) .... Salomón Stramer
Francis (amiga de Willy) .... Paulina Tajman
Sr. Harold Wagner .... Leonidas Sokoloff
Standley (mozo de café) .... Isujer Handfuss
Jenny (Secretaria de Charlie) ... Elsa Ravinovich
Una señorita .... Margot Steinberg
Otra señorita .... Berta Ais
Un cliente .... Pedro Fischman

Director de orquesta: Simón Tenovsky
Escenografía: Casa Hornos   Sastrería: Casa Schneider
Peluquería: Garde   Utilería: Otonello   Apuntador: T. Liberson
Traspunte: Pedro Fischman

PRECIO DE LAS LOCALIDADES
(Sábado Noche, Domingo Noche y Feriados Noche)

	Precio	Ley 13.487	Total
Fila 1 a 12	$ 13.50	1.30	14.80
Fila 13 a 16	,, 10.50	1.—	11.50
Fila 17 a 20	,, 7.50	0.70	8.20
Fila 21 a 25	,, 5.50	0.50	6.—
Superpullman	,, 5.50	0.50	6.—
Pullman	,, 3.50	0.30	3.80
Ent. Palco	,, 9.10	0.90	10.—
Palco Bajo 4 ent.	,, 60.—	6.—	66.—
Menores	,, 1.80	0.20	2.—

GOLDBERG & JACOBS
PARKWAY THEATRE
Eastern Parkway at St. Johns Pl. B'klyn DI 5-1390

Goldberg and Jacobs present
JOSEPH BULOFF
IN
ARTHUR MILLER'S
Death of A Salesman
with Luba Kadison

A Play in 2 Acts, Staged by Joseph Buloff

Music by Yasha Kreitzberg. Settings by Saltzman Bros.

THE CAST IN ORDER OF THEIR APPEARANCE:

WILLY LOMAN .... JOSEPH BULOFF
LINDA .... LUBA KADISON
BILL .... LEWIS NORMAN
HARRY .... YOKOB SUSONOFF
BERNARD .... DAVID ELLIN
THE WOMAN .... SONIA ZOMINA
CHARLEY .... SAM GERTLER
UNCLE BEN .... NATHAN GOLDBERG
HOWARD WAGNER .... MAX ROSENBLATT
JENNY .... JENNIE CASHER
STANLEY .... DAVID DANK
MISS FORSYTHE .... HARIETTE ROLLINS
LETTA .... THELMA JACOBS

Stage Manager — David Dank

גאָלדבערג און דזשייקאָבס פרעזענטירן
יוסף בולאָוו
אין ארטור מיללער'ס
טויט פון א סעילסמאן
מיט ליובא קאדיסאָן
א דראמא אין 2 אקטן
רעזשי, יוסף בולאָוו

מוזיק - יאשא קרייצבערג - דעקאָראציעס פון זאלצמאן ברידער

פערזאָנען לויט זייער דערשיינונג :

וויליע לאָמאן ....יוסף בולאָוו
לינדא.............................ליובא קאדיסאָן
בילל............................לואיס נאָרמאן
הערארי............................יאקאָב סוזאנאָוו
בערנארד ....דוד עללין
די פרוי............................סאָניא זאָמינע
משארלי............................סעם גערטלער
אָנקעל בען ....ניימען גאָלדבערג
האָווארד וואגנער ....מאקס ראָזענבלאט
דזשעני ....דזשעני קעשיער
סטענלי............................דוד דענק
מיסס פאָרסייט ....העריעט ראָלינס
לעטטא ....טהעלמא דזשייקאָבס

ביהנע פארוואלטער — דוד דענק

Programs of productions of A. Miller's Death of a Salesman, *starring Joseph Buloff. Left: Buenos Aires, 1949; right: Brooklyn, 1951.*

Buloff on the American Stage

Before Buloff became one of the few foreign-born and foreign-trained Jewish actors who successfully made the transition to the English-language American stage and cinema, he took part in several other notable events in the Yiddish Theatre of the 1930's. On our return from a most rewarding Argentine tour, we learned that Maurice Schwartz had gone to Poland, leaving the large theatre at Second Avenue and 12th Street vacant, and that its owner, with the Hebrew Actors Union, wished to reopen it with a season of plays. We were invited to form a company for the purpose. Buloff and I accepted the offer and opened with a play that had premiered and had been well-received in Buenos Aires: *The 60,000 Heroes*, by Benjamin Ressler. It proved less successful in New York.

However, we rounded out a generally propitious season with *The Verdict*, Artzybashev's *Jealousy* and *Parnoseh*, by Notte Gottesfeld. The following year, after Schwartz's return, Buloff moved into a smaller theatre further down on Second Avenue, where he presented his own Yiddish translations of Pirandello's *He, She and the Ox*, with Baratov as co-star.

In the mid-1930's, Buloff moved on to Broadway. His first English-language role was in *Don't Look Now*, produced by Gustave Blum in November 1936, which lasted only sixteen performances.

The following year, Michael Todd—honoring earlier promises—starred Joe in *Call Me Ziggy*, and then in *The Man from Cairo* in 1938. As Todd's first Broadway productions, these were not quite successful even though they earned Buloff excellent press notices. But Michael Todd was not discouraged and went on to become a top movie and stage producer.

On the strength of the high critical acclaim for Buloff personally, a New York agent arranged for a screen test in Hollywood. The ensuing three-night train ride, his exhaustion upon arrival in Los Angeles, the flunky at the railroad station who whisked him on to the studio in a limousine, and the screen test itself—in which he desperately tried to show only his right profile, as he was acutely self-conscious of a wartime scar on his left cheek—all these and more became favorite topics of reminiscence for Joe in the years to come. After the test, he was handed a train ticket and sent back to New York. A few days later, he ran into his agent on Broadway, who asked: "Why are you here? You're supposed to be in California."

"They turned me down," said Joe.

"They can't do that to us," the agent exploded. "Come to my office with me, and I'll get to the bottom of this." A long-distance telephone call was placed, and a powerful studio executive was asked what had happened to the Buloff test.

"What sort of an actor did you send us?" he exclaimed. "On the right side, he photographs like a matinee idol. On the left, he looks like a gangster."

"So you are getting two actors for the price of one," the agent replied.

"But neither of them speaks English," the executive snapped back. This was only a temporary setback, however. In the late thirties, Buloff was signed by RKO for featured roles in *Let's Make Music* with Bob Crosby, Bing's brother; and in *They Met in Argentina*, with Maureen O'Hara and a Rodgers-and-Hart score. After both RKO films were released to lukewarm receptions in 1941, Buloff wrote the following disenchanted letter to a fellow actor:

Dear Lew:

Yesterday I was delighted to see myself in *They Met in Argentina.* Given the confusion and the mood of defeatism during the shooting of the picture, I was most pleasantly surprised to find my sour puss so entertainingly dominant. In fact, nearly all the laughs that could be squeezed out of this dry cane were credited by the audience to me.

On the way home, another of my adventures in Hollywood films began rolling in my head. I recalled *Malvina Swings It,*★ my introduction to movieland fantasy, in which I was expected to make bullets out of cream cheese. After being patted on the shoulder and promised that my unsatisfactory part would be changed, I found it was indeed, but in name only: a switch from cream cheese to Limburger.

Then came the fiasco of *Argentina.* After I saw the director collapse, the producer fired and the picture shelved, I felt that there was nothing left for me but to return to my old horse and buggy, with little hope of ever resurfacing in the golden inferno called Hollywood.

★ Shooting title for *Let's Make Music.*

Joseph Buloff as William Auchinschloss (right) and C. Aubrey Smith as Halstead Carter in production of I. Leighton and B. Block's Spring Again, *New York, 1941.*

But now that *Argentina* has been auspiciously reborn, I have new hope of being rediscovered under some heap of dust called *Let's Make Nothing* or *They Met Nowhere.*

Hope to see you soon.

Sincerely,
Buloff

Buloff's hopes for better opportunities in the movies were realized in the mid-1950's with his appearance in two MGM productions: *Somebody Up There Likes Me*, a screen version of the autobiography of boxer Rocky Graziano—which proved to be a box-office success and brought Paul Newman to stardom—and *Silk Stockings*, in which Buloff played a Soviet Russian commissar. The latter picture, a remake of *Ninotchka*, had a Cole Porter score and starred Fred Astaire and Cyd Charisse. It is still shown on late-night television.

In the early 1940's, Buloff's American stage career took a definite turn for the better. He appeared in *Spring Again*, which ran through 241 performances on Broadway (1941-42). Produced and directed by Gutherie McClintick, it starred C. Aubrey Smith and Grace George as a squabbling literary couple, happily reconciling at a birthday party in the final scene. While Buloff's function was solely as an actor (playing a sharp Hollywood producer), he indulged his penchant for constructive directorial suggestions to improve the production, and gave McClintick

Joseph Buloff in production of J. Fields and J. Chodorov's My Sister
Eileen, *New York, 1942.*

the idea to bring the final curtain down with a bang by having
a Western Union messenger deliver a singing birthday telegram. As revealed by Kirk Douglas in his autobiography, the
movie-star-to-be made his first Broadway appearance as that
singing messenger. What Douglas does not mention in his
book, probably because he does not even know it, is that his
lucky break came as a result of Buloff's imaginative conception.

Joe's next role was in *My Sister Eileen*, and thereafter came the
Ali Hakim part in the Theatre Guild's smash musical hit
Oklahoma!. When he wrote to me during the out-of-town
tryouts, he was less than optimistic about the play's chances for
a long run. Yet *Oklahoma!* opened in March 1943 and ran for
five years and 2,200 performances on Broadway. While in the
original cast, Alfred Drake, Joan Roberts, Celeste Holm and
Howard Da Silva had singing roles, Buloff's part as the peddler
Ali Hakim was mainly a speaking one. When he did have a
number to sing, he carried it off in his own peculiar half-singing,
half-speaking style.

When, years later, Rex Harrison sang-spoke his way through
the lead in *My Fair Lady*, someone asked him how he had
learned the technique. He is reported to have replied, "I picked
it up by watching Joe Buloff in *Oklahoma!*."

At the time of his performance in *Oklahoma!*, Buloff had
an unrelated but memorable encounter with Shlomo Michoels,
actor and director at the
Moscow Jewish Art The-
atre, which he later re-
corded in his own inimi-
table fashion.

*Joseph Buloff in production of R.
Rodgers'* Oklahoma!, *New York,
1943.*

Buloff's Michoels Story

Among the great directors of the Jewish stage whom I have known, I count Leib Kadison of the Vilna Troupe, Morris Schwartz of the Yiddish Art Theatre and Shlomo Michoels of the Moscow State Yiddish Art Theatre. I performed under the first two and met Michoels under curious circumstances during World War II.

In 1943 he came from the USSR to the United States on an official mission: funds-and-sympathy solicitation from the Jewish community for the Soviet war effort. Instead of being welcomed as an ally—as he had presumably expected—he immediately faced a boycott organized by the *Daily Forward*, which had not forgiven the many wrongs inflicted on the Jewish people by the Stalinists, including the 1939 Hitler-Stalin pact and the execution of Bundist leaders Erlich and Alter. The influential *Forward* passed the word to the Hebrew Actors Union that there was to be no participation by its members in any official welcomes or receptions for Michoels and his party.

The prospect of failure prompted him to telephone me. Why me of all people? At the time, I was appearing with the original cast in *Oklahoma!,* and some astute person in the theatre had apparently informed Michoels that I had made the transition to the American stage, was not beholden to the Hebrew Actors Union, and would be free to give him independent aid and advice.

While I understood and even sympathized with The *Forward*'s viewpoint, I also knew that the Russian people were staunch allies of the United States and formidable fighters against the Nazis, who were murdering the Jews of Europe. Impetuously, I decided to help Michoels and arranged to meet him at his midtown hotel.

When I knocked, Michoels himself opened the door. I was instantly struck by his bizarre appearance. He was slightly shorter than I am, and had a bare, bulging brow and jutting jaws to match. His sagging, shapeless trousers were held up by a cord around his waist, and his worn-out, tieless shirt was open at the neck. In short, his appearance was entirely appropriate to the grotesquely anti-bourgeoise style for which his Moscow Yiddish Art Theatre was noted.

There was one other man in the room, a heavy Slavic type, who said nothing but remained in his chair, ostensibly reading a Russian newspaper that almost concealed his face. I figured him for a GPU agent.

Michoels spoke in voluble Russian as he imparted to me his eagerness to reach the Jewish theatre community and his failure to date to get any kind of cooperation. I said to him: "Gospodin Michoels, there is no way you can move The *Forward* or the Hebrew Actors Union. So here is what you should do: Rent a hall and announce a forthcoming lecture by you on the history and theory of your Moscow State Yiddish Art Theatre. The Jewish actors of New York will surely attend. Their union can control their employment conditions, but it cannot restrict their right as American citizens to attend a public lecture."

Michoels embraced me Russian-style as he proclaimed: "We'll do it! You are a genius." Two days later, he delivered his lecture. I attended it and so did almost every other Yiddish actor in town. In a packed hotel ballroom Michoels held his audience spellbound with reminiscences about the founding and the ups and downs of his famous theatre.

At the conclusion, he again hailed me as a public relations expert and his first friend in America. Responding in kind, I congratulated him on his lecture and invited him to see me in *Oklahoma!,* and afterwards backstage.

Sure enough, Michoels attended the play that evening and then visited me in my dressing room. I changed into a white linen suit befitting the warm summer weather, with shoes and shirt to match, and a solid-blue silk cravat. Once more mutual praise was lavished—he swore I was the best actor in *Oklahoma!*—and I invited him out for a drink. Since he was still dressed like a muzhik, I elected to take him downtown, to the Fifth Avenue Hotel bar in Greenwich Village, where I hoped his unconventional attire would pass without notice.

It wasn't so much his clothes that drew attention as the way he drank. We both ordered straight vodka, which the waiter brought in shot glasses. I took my drink, but my guest protested.

"I don't drink from eyedroppers," he scoffed. "Tell the comrade waiter to bring me a real glass of vodka."

So the waiter brought him a water glass filled with Smirnoff's best, and Michoels proceeded to down it exactly as if it were water. We went on to match drink for drink; that is, I took sips from shot glasses while he bottomed-up whole tumblers.

Shortly his Weltschmertz dissolved, and he embarked on a recitation of his future plan: He was going to Washington the next day for an official reception at the State Department and a tour of the capital. Then he was to return to New York for a Madison Square Garden rally sponsored by the Soviet-American Friendship Society. Then back to Moscow.

"When the war is over," he said, "a grateful government will build me a magnificent new theatre. And you, my new-found friend and great actor, will be invited there as a star. You will play Andreyev, Chekhov, Molière, Shakespeare, Ansky, Pinsky—and the Russian public will adore you."

Having once gotten my head out of the Russian bear's embrace, I hardly intended to put it back there again. But I said nothing.

When closing time came, we walked out on lower Fifth Avenue. Although the city was blacked out, a full moon illuminated the grandest avenue in the greatest city in the world. Reacting to the beauty of the setting—not to mention the reflected glow and emanating warmth from the consumed vodka—I found myself expansively saying: "Listen, Comrade, tomorrow you are going to Washington to represent your great country. Would it be right and proper for you to appear there in sagging pants and a torn shirt, without even a tie? I'll tell you what: I have a closet full of suits, stacks of shirts—colored and white alike—and a wide selection of ties. Come home with me, and I will outfit you from head to toe, well enough to meet even President Roosevelt himself."

Evidently, I had said the wrong thing, for Michoels suddenly turned hostile. Pulling out a pile of U.S. currency that could have rendered a Cossack brigade breathless, he growled: "You louse, you so-and-so, you think I don't have money, do you? My government has provided me with enough funds. But I refuse to spend the workers' money on your bourgeois trappings. I spit on your lackey cravats and white suits! Let your president see me as I am, a Soviet proletarian dressed like the people!" And he abruptly strode away from me.

Well, ours proved to be a short-lived friendship, I concluded; and, determined to forget all about Michoels, I went home to sleep off the effect of the unusual-for-me intake of alcohol. But I was destined to see the man one more time, under yet more strained circumstances.

On his return from Washington, his participation in a Soviet-American Friendship rally was publicly announced and, to my surprise, I, too, was invited to appear in it. Friends advised me that, since I had ostensibly championed Michoels, a refusal on my part to make an appearance would create adverse publicity, and that I therefore ought not to decline.

Again attired as befits a leading man in the capitalist theatre, I entered Madison Square Garden's crowded arena and was again possessed of serious doubts as Uncle Joe (Stalin) looked down on me from his two-story-high portrait on the wall.

Every leftist in town was there. I realized that I had strayed into a Communist rally but nonetheless performed my piece to loud applause, and sat down to await Michoel's appearance.

He did a humorous sketch by Sholom Aleichem—one which I myself had frequently done—about a Jew and a Russian-Orthodox priest trapped together on a runaway train in the early days of railroading. Through combined efforts—their ignorance of mechanics and repeated blunders notwithstanding—they succeed in stopping the locomotive and saving their lives. Whereupon the two men—though the priest is a rabid anti-Semite—recognize each other's essential dignity and humanity.

As he read in beautiful Yiddish, Michoels elicited roars of happy laughter. But that was only a beginning, for when he had finished with Sholom Aleichem's text, he went on to add his own coda:

"At this very moment, even as I speak to you, a Soviet Tiger-Tank is rolling across the steppes. At the controls are a Jewish soldier and a Gentile soldier—descendants perhaps of Sholom Aleichem's very same Jew and priest. But unlike those two, our soldiers know their machine. And they drive, they maneuver, they fire their weapons, they fight on and on against the brutal Nazi invaders. They are battling and winning—Jew and Gentile together—for a free Soviet, for a free world!"

The audience rose, roaring. But Michoels was still not finished.

"The other day," he continued, when he had managed to make himself heard, "the other day, an American dandy of an actor came to me and said, 'Michoels, why are you in rags? Come, let me dress you like a fancy American, in a white linen suit and a blue silk tie.' And I, as a proud Soviet Citizen, said, 'Never.'"

He then pointed to the gigantic photomural of Stalin and added: "And I say to you, my friends, blessed be the hand that keeps us in rags, so that we may buy tanks and guns and bullets to fight for our homeland and kill the damned Fascist aggressors."

At this point, the audience went absolutely berserk. Some climbed up the walls; others jumped off the balconies. Still others banged their heads against the seats in an ecstasy of enthusiasm.

As for me, I waited for the final blow. I was sure that Michoels would name me as the capitalist lackey who had offended him, the true proletarian artist; at which point the audience would have trampled me to death, for sure.

Fortunately, Michoels refrained from identifying me and I departed in one piece. It was the last time I saw him, but I heard about him later.

He returned to Russia, where he was briefly permitted to reopen his theatre after the war. Then, as Stalin's anti-Semitism grew blatant, his cast was reportedly arrested one by one, and finally the Moscow State Yiddish Art Theatre was abolished. Next, he was ordered to attend a performance in Minsk, where he was taken from his hotel, beaten to death and left in the snow.

Thus perished Michoels, slain by the hand he had blessed.

Buloff's Later Career

Though Joe grew increasingly restless in the part of Ali Hakim in *Oklahoma!*, he filled it for over three years, longer than any other of the main players in the original. He needed the money, for he now had a little daughter and a big apartment, and his wife had temporarily suspended any income-earning theatre work to take care of the child.

When he finally ended his engagement, he took the lead in *The Whole World Over*, which was directed by Harold Clurman and featured Uta Hagen. Other Broadway plays in which he appeared included *To Quito and Back*, a Theatre-Guild Production by Ben Hecht; *The Fifth Season*, a garment-center comedy, in which he succeeded Menasha Skulnik and which subsequently toured the United States and England; *The Wall*, starring George C. Scott and based on John Hersey's novel about the Warsaw Ghetto uprising; and *Morning Star*, with Molly Picon.

In 1952 Buloff directed Helen Hayes in *Mrs. McThing*, a surprise hit by Mary Chase, produced by ANTA. He received the assignment through Clurman, who one evening had brought the producer Robert Whitehead

Joseph Buloff as Aaron Greenspan and Molly Picon as Becky Felderman in production of S. Regan's Morning Star, *New York, 1940.*

Jospeh Buloff as Zamiano in B. Hecht's To Quito and Back, *New York, 1937.*

to Joe's Folksbiene revival of *The Singer of His Sorrow*. As a result, Whitehead determined that Buloff was the only man capable of directing Mrs. Chase's fantasy. Buloff made several key revisions in the script that helped to earn *Mrs. McThing* 350 performances on Broadway as well as numerous revivals. Like most actors, including top-ranking figures, Buloff had periods of "liberty" from Broadway. Unlike most, however, he had other outlets for his talents. As a virtual pioneer in TV drama, he appeared on the Philco Playhouse (NBC) in *The Reluctant Citizen*, in Paddy Chayefsky's *Holiday Song* and in other plays. He also played in a situation-comedy series, "Two Girls Named Smith," and as Mr. Pincus, proprietor of Pincus Pines and Pincus Palms, in Molly Berg's "The Goldbergs." He was always in demand as a reader of Yiddish classics and as a lecturer on Jewish theatre, appearing before colleges, symposia, synagogues, fraternal organizations, and festivals across the country. Most satisfying for him were his extensive tours of Uruguay, Mexico, Brazil, Argentina, England, France and, most important, Israel.

Although justifiably proud of his achievements in the American theater, Buloff never forgot his origins as a Yiddish actor. As he once remarked, "I made money on the American stage and buried it in the Yiddish Theatre."

Thus, he directed H. Leivick's play about political prisoners in Russia, *Chains*, for ARTEF. With Folksbiene, he revived *The Brothers Ashkenazi*, and *The Singer of His Sorrow*.

In the early 1970's he joined producer Rothpearl in staging a Yiddish version of *The Fifth Season* and in the revival of *Hard To Be a Jew*.

Joseph Buloff as Feodor Vorontsov and Uta Hagen as Olga Vorontsov in K. Simonov's The Whole World Over, *New York, 1947.*

THE ZIONIST RECORD, FRIDAY, NOVEMBER 11, 1955.

THE MAGIC OF BULOFF

Let us not discuss whether "The Fifth Season" by Sylvia Regan is a realistic or even a good play. The important thing is that it is good theatre and gives us a chance to see a really top-class actor from America.

Joseph Buloff has all the tricks of the trade—theatrical and, according to the play, also sartorial —at his finger tips. He also has a few more dodges than most fine comic actors. He can be lovable and grotesque at the same time.

He can do absurd things that— once you have come under his influence — seem as natural as smiling.

Even he, it must be admitted, has to have time to make the first act of this farce about a clothing factory interesting and amusing. By the end of Act I, he has us thinking there is nothing funny about this dress business except Buloff. By the end of Act II, he has us believing that there is nothing more entertaining than girl and money tangles—if they involve Buloff. By the end of the third act his drolleries seem enchanting, the story almost gripping, "The Fifth Season" a vital matter — and we know by then that Buloff is brilliant.

It is no slight on the rest of the cast to say that they do not come anywhere near the standard required to partner this expert. Who could? Their voices, movements, emotions, all seem stagey beside his. The curious thing is that they are acting almost "straight" while he is indulging almost continuously in antics. That is superlative art.

The partner (Norman Lane), who loves his wife (Gertrude Miles) and falls for his model (Valerie Philip), is a more true-to-life character than Max Pincus (Joseph Buloff), who takes the blame and saves everybody from disaster, including himself. Yet he looks unreal beside him. The girls borrowed from the firm upstairs whenever a buyer is expected are as lovely to look at as the frocks, yet they seem unimportant beside this ugly little fellow with the winning smile and the half-closed eyes.

Miles Lewis, the chainstore tycoon, is a character of celluloid and could hardly be made more plausible than does Harold Lake, but even Miriam Oppenheim (Beryl Gordon) takes on life only when the warmth of the little sallow tailor's personality radiates upon her.

Good performances come also from Martin Cowen, James Russell and Rita Kay (when she isn't overdoing it), but no one really counts beside Buloff.

From Joseph Buloff's international tours: South Africa—clipping from the Johannesburg newspaper The Zionist Record *on Joseph Buloff's performance in S. Regan's* The Fifth Season, *1955; Uruguay—program from production of* Diary of Anne Frank, *starring Joseph Buloff, Montevideo, 1957; France— program of recitations by Joseph Buloff and Luba Kadison, Paris, 1948.*

S. O. D. R. E.
ESTUDIO AUDITORIO
MERCEDES Y ANDES   MONTEVIDEO

LUNES 16 y MARTES 17 DE SETIEMBRE DE 1957
a las 22 horas

UNICAS 2 FUNCIONES
auspiciadas por el
INSTITUTO CULTURAL "URUGUAY - ISRAEL"
Consejo Ejecutivo

Presidente: Prof. CARLOS SABAT ERCASTY.
Vice-Presidentes: Prof. Oscar Secco Ellauri (Ministro de Relaciones Exteriores), Dr. Jacobo Hazan.
Secretarios: Escr. Ernesto D. Guerrini, Sr. Eduardo Correa Aguirre.
Pro-Secretario: Sr. Nelson Pilossof.
Tesorero: Sr. Miguel Krell.
Pro-Tesorero: Q. I. Aristides Santerini.
Consejeros: Arq. Leopoldo C. Agorio, Dr. Jaime Bayley, Dr. Luis Alberto Brause, Dr. Arturo J. Dubra, Prof. Francisco Espínola, Prof. Hugo Fernández Artucio, Dr. Antonio G. Fusco, Dr. Héctor Grauert, Sr. Eduardo Lezama, Dr. Armando R. Malet, Dr. Emilio Oribe, Dr. Héctor Paysee Reyes, Sr. Jorge Paez Vilaró, Dr. Dardo Regules, Prof. Carlos Sabat Pebet, Ing. Edmundo Sisto, Sr. Adolfo Tejera.
Oficial de Enlace entre la Legación de Israel y el Instituto: Agregado Sr. Nessim Isaac.
Vocales: Sr. Mario J. Tissoni Estapé, Dra. Lea Lestieri de Scazzocchio, Sr. José Wainstein.

STRAMER - FELDBAUM - NAREPKI
presentan al eminente actor

JOSEPH BULOFF
-- EN --

El Diario de Ana Frank

En 2 partes teatralizado por FRANCES GOODRICH y ALBERT HACKET
Traducción en idish: LUBA KADISON
Dirección: **JOSEPH BULOFF**

REPARTO:

Señor Frank ...... Joseph Buloff	Señora Frank ..... Clara Stramer
Miep .... Ana Feldbaum	Margot Frank ..... Ana Lang
Señora Van Dan ..... Eni Liton	Ana Frank .... Dora Windler
Señor Van Dan .. Israel Feldbaum	Kroller .... Salomón Stramer
Peter .... Pinjas Apel	Dusel .... Jacobo Denker

La acción se desarrolla durante la segunda guerra mundial y luego, en Amsterdam.

Apuntador: JOSE LIBERSON   Traspunte: FELIX LEVEN
Escenografía: JOAQUIN PEREZ ejecutados en casa HORNOS
Efectos de sonido: CASA MILRUD

Por disposición del Consejo Departamental, todos los espectadores con la sola excepción de las damas que ocupan palcos, deberán permanecer con la cabeza descubierta durante el desarrollo del espectáculo.
Por disposición de la Ordenanza de Prevención y Defensa contra el Fuego, al terminar el espectáculo el público podrá abandonar la sala por cualquier puerta de salida. En caso de "alarma" conserve la serenidad, no corra y tenga presente la salida más próxima al sector que ocupa.
Por disposición municipal, no se podrá entrar a la sala una vez comenzado el espectáculo.

PRECIOS DE LAS LOCALIDADES

Palcos con 6 Entradas	$ 60.00	Galería Baja 1ª fila	" 6.00
Plateas de Fila 1 a 15	" 10.00	Galería Baja otras filas	" 4.00
Plateas otras filas	" 8.00	Galería Alta 1ª fila	" 4.00
Tertulia 1ª fila	" 9.00	Galería Alta otras filas	" 3.00
Tertulia otras filas	" 7.00	Entrada general numerada	" 2.00

Agradecemos a los Sres. Otto Frank, Dr. L. de Young, Sra. Lidia Vinkell y al "Instituto Holandés de Documentos de Guerra" de Amsterdam, la ayuda y asesoría que han facilitado para el montaje de
EL DIARIO DE ANA FRANK

Imp. Margulies - Andes 1146

זאל גאווא

שבת, דעם 16-טן אקטאבער 1948
.היאם פרעזענטירט

יוסף בולאוו
און
ליובא קאדיסאן

אין א
ווארט-קאנצערט

SALLE GAVEAU
SAMEDI LE 16 OCTOBRE 1948
•
sous la présidence d'Honneur d'H. I. A. S.
•
SOIRÉE ARTISTIQUE
DE
JOSEPH BULOFF
ET
LIUBA KADISON
MONOLOGUES ET POÈMES

Poster from production of O. Dimov's Singer of His Sorrow, *London, 1948; starring Joseph Buloff and Luba Kadison.*

S T A G E B I L L
Chicago's Theatre Magazine
Season 1959-1960

THE INSPECTOR GENERAL
Starring
JOSEPH BULOFF
GOODMAN MEMORIAL THEATRE

Twenty-first Season   *1968 - 1969*

**Jewish Community Center
of Cleveland**

PRESENTS

JOSEPH BULOFF

IN

SEIDMAN AND SON

By ELICK MOLL

Playing nightly, except Fridays and Mondays, through December 1, 1968
Curtain — 8:30 p.m. nightly; 7:30 p.m. Sunday

BLANCHE R. HALLE THEATRE
3505 Mayfield Road

PLAYHOUSE *on the Mall*
ROBERT LUDLUM
PRODUCER

Bergen Mall Shopping Center • Route 4 • Paramus, N. J.

July 20 - August 1, 1965

**SAM   GLORIA   JOSEPH
LEVENE   DE HAVEN   BULOFF**
in
"FIDELIO"

Section Two—SUNDAY NEWS, APRIL 15, 1962

Clipping from the New York Sunday News, *April 15, 1962, on Joseph Buloff in* A Chekhov Sketchbook.

ACTOR'S HOLIDAY ● *Joseph Buloff is all over the place in "A Chekhov Sketchbook," triple bill at the Gramercy Arts. Top to bottom, he's seen as a prisoner in "The Vagrant," an aged sexton in "The Witch" and a customer in "The Music Shop." Helen Waren is the bellringer, Frank C. Borgman the music dealer.*

Program from the 1962 Tel-Aviv production of A Chekhov Sketchbook; *Joseph Buloff as a prisoner in* The Vagrant.

Reviewing *Hard To Be a Jew* in the November 19, 1973, issue of *The Nation*, Harold Clurman praised the endearing quality of Sholom Aleichem's comedy, the songs of Sholom Secunda, the choreography of Pearl Lang and the cast in general. He saved his highest accolades, however, for the star, postulating unequivocally: "Buloff is one of the most brilliant actors in the world."

To justify so bold a statement, the famous critic devoted two columns to the art of Joseph Buloff, saying, among other things:

"One imagines Buloff as a descendant of the *commedia del'arte* tradition. Everything in him dances; his body, his hands, his fingers, his face, his voice . . . . He seems agile even when standing still. But he rarely stands still; he is constantly in motion even when the movement is so minute that we feel rather than see it." Clurman noted that Buloff's motions seem to "weave, flutter, twist, turn and fly."

"His gestures speak, describe, sing; they are artfully dramatic; they provide graphic meaning and commentary. They convey the nervous eloquence of a suppressed but irrepressible people."

The Nation's drama critic went on to enumerate Buloff's portrayals of a professor in *The Whole World Over*, a detective in a play by Felicien Marosau, and a petty merchant in *Hard To Be a Jew*. In Buloff's interpretation of these varied roles, he found that "there is always a trace of person somehow out of place, self-protective through shrewdness and imagination, a lovable scamp. If he is not always reliable and respectable, it is because the world has forced him into a corner where he defends himself with something like genius and with the humor of one who has passed beyond the need to hope because for him life is enough, no matter how much mischief and travail he may find in it."

Clurman concluded: "Buloff is an artist; an uncommon phenomenon among actors."

Perhaps Buloff's greatest renown on the English-language stage came as an interpreter of Arthur Miller roles. Apart from the highly acclaimed Yiddish version of *Death of a Salesman*, he established a closer rapport with Miller's characters when in the 1970's he went on to play Gregory Solomon, the 89-year-old furniture dealer in Miller's *The Price*. The part was developed by him on a tour of Florida and perfected on a national tour.

When Buloff was close to his eightieth birthday, we went to see our friend Joseph Wiseman in a play at the Harold Clurman Theatre. Backstage, we were introduced to the producer, Jack Garfein, who within minutes expressed eagerness to star Joe in a play to be selected later. Garfein agreed, at my suggestion, to a revival of *The Price*, and the rest is history. Buloff as Gregory Solomon was surrounded by a top-notch cast: Fritz Weaver, Michael Ryan and Scotty Bloch. Miller attended the dress rehearsal with Garfein. At the point in the play where Solomon boasts that members of his profession, furniture appraisers, are respected "like doctors," Joe ad-libbed: "We are respected like doctors—used to be."

FOLKSBIENE · · · PLAYHOUSE

175 East Broadway, New York, N. Y. 10002

Phone: AL 4-2211

Presents

JOSEPH BULOFF

in

"The Brothers Ashkenazi"

based on the novel by

I. J. SINGER

adopted by

LUBA KADISON

GALA OPENING

on Saturday, October 31st, 1970
166

Program from the Folksbiene Playhouse production of I.J. Singer's The Brothers Ashkenazi, *New York, 1970; starring Joseph Buloff as Max Ashkenazi.*

Joseph Buloff as Gregory Solomon in
A. Miller's The Price.

Aware as he was that Miller frowned upon any change in his play's lines, Garfein nervously glanced at him, only to observe the celebrated playwright chuckling as he mumbled to himself: "Genius, sheer genius."

The critics were unanimous in their acclaim of both the revival production of *The Price* and Buloff's performance in it. To accommodate the crowds that flocked to the small Clurman Theatre, Garfein had to move the play onto a Broadway stage. He also took the performance to Menotti's Festival of Two Worlds in Charleston, South Carolina.

The next season, we revived our *Chekhov Sketchbook* at the Harold Clurman. Buloff had to concede that at age eighty he could not risk the strain of taking the lead in all three one-acters, and he appeared in only the final piece, *In the Music Shop*.

Another chance to show his undiminished acting skills came to him in his eighth decade when Warren Beatty took him on location to Finland and England for the filming of *Reds*. Buloff delivered a vivid cameo performance as a revolutionary who befriends journalist John Reed (played by Beatty) and his wife (played by Diane Keaton) on a train to Petrograd. *Reds* was Buloff's last film.

However, he was not through with the theatre or with *The Price*. He repeated the role of Gregory Solomon when the American Jewish Theatre revived the play at the 92nd Street Y. As a result of its success, the play was taken to the Festival of Israel in 1983. Unfortunately, Joe could not undertake the trip because of failing health.

He had so wanted to return to the land where he had found his most appreciative and enthusiastic audiences. A warm welcome had been prepared for him, including an award from Tel-Aviv University for his contribution to Israeli theatre over a period of forty years (from the 1940's through the 1970's). The director of the American Jewish Theatre accepted the award for him, as Buloff was honored in absentia.

A subsequent trip to California for a reading engagement that Joe insisted on making further aggravated his physical condition. He passed away on February 27, 1985.

In recognition of his unique artistry, a memorial for Joseph Buloff was held at the Clurman Theatre on West 42nd Street thirty days after his death. The theatre was packed; many mourners had to stand in the aisles. Among those who paid tribute to Joe were Fritz Weaver, who had co-starred with him in *The Price*; Celeste Holm, a leading member of the original *Oklahoma!* cast; producer Jack Garfein; Dr. Joseph C. Landis of Queens College; Jack Rechtzeit, president of the Hebrew Actors Union; producer Joseph Papp; Abe Feder; Azaria Rapaport; and Joseph Wiseman.

An oversize photo of Buloff in his role as Gregory Solomon in *The Price* hung on the backdrop. As the speakers evoked his sixty years in the theatre, Joe's portrait began to tilt, twist and sway. The audience gasped; all eyes were on the suddenly animated image of Buloff.

Reporting on the event in the *New York Times* of March 31, 1985, Irving Howe commented: "Again, Joe Buloff has upstaged them all."

Last portrait of Joseph Buloff, 1983
(© Nancy Rica Schiff, 1983).

Israel

Buloff left an imposing archive of theatre memorabilia. Over the years, some items from the collection were given to the YIVO Institute for Jewish Research, to the New York Public Library's Performing Arts Branch at Lincoln Center, and to Tel-Aviv University. After Buloff's death, Barbara and I, concerned that Buloff's archive be preserved and accessible for future generations, presented the entire collection to the Harvard College Library. In appreciation of the gift, Harvard held an exhibit of the Joseph Buloff Archives at Cambridge in September of 1987. The brochure announcing the event, by Dr. Charles Berlin, curator of the Judaica Collection, referred to Joe as "an artist in two worlds"—an apt description, for Buloff had made the transition to the American stage while loyally remaining in and of the Yiddish Theatre.

Deep in his heart he knew that Jewish drama was the source of his unique artistry and the truest outlet for his thespian and directorial talents. From the 1940's on, he found his best Yiddish audience in Israel, which therefore merits a special chapter.

ההסתדרות הכללית של העובדים העברים בארץ-ישראל

מועצת פועלי ת"א-יפו   המחלקה לתרבות ולנוער
הועד המחוזי לאיגוד עובדי המדינה – ועדת התרבות

אולם **אהל שם**   הופעה מיוחדת לעובדי המדינה   ביום חמישי כ"ב אייר תשי"ג 7. 5. 1953

יוסף בולוף

השחקן היהודי-האמריקאי המפורסם
ההתחלה בשעה 8.30 בערב

כרטיסים במחיר: 550; 700; 750 פר' בבית ברנר, חדר 43 מיום 29.4.53 בשעות 7–5 בערב.

Poster announcing Joseph Buloff's "special appearance for state workers," Tel-Aviv, 1953.

Joseph Buloff as Tevye in Sholom Aleichem's Tevye and His Seven Daughters, *Tel-Aviv, 1961.*

Joseph Buloff as Gideon (left) and Shimon Finkel in P. Chayefsky's Gideon, *Tel-Aviv, 1967 (© I.P.P.A. Ltd./Photo Macky).*

Joseph Buloff as Max Ashkenazi in I.J. Singer's The Brothers Ashkenazi, *Tel-Aviv, 1966 (© I.P.P.A. Ltd./Photo Macky).*

Buloff was introduced to Israel in 1945 (before it officially became the Jewish State) by Misha Elman. When the famous concert violinist was touring there, his agent asked him to recommend other performers, and he mentioned his friend Buloff. Without further ado, asking no questions, the agent engaged Joe and sent him an airline ticket to Israel.

On meeting him at Lod Airport, the first question the agent asked Joe was, "Where is your instrument?"

"Here," Buloff replied, pointing to his throat.

"A singer?" the agent asked.

"No, I read Yiddish poems and stories."

The surprised agent expressed doubts over the reception of such recitals by a largely Hebrew-speaking Israeli public but booked Buloff for a few performances in Tel Aviv and a tour of kibbutzim and schools. He need not have worried. Buloff's lively recitations of poems by Manger and Leivick, and of stories by Sholom Aleichem and Peretz, made him an instant hit. Though Hebrew is the dominant language in the land, thousands of recent settlers whose mother tongue was Yiddish flocked to hear it beautifully articulated by a master artist. Sweltering in packed auditoriums or sitting on hard benches in open fields, they responded to his performances, to his voice and gestures, with laughter, tears and applause.

During the tour, Buloff chanced to meet a producer, Pavel Gorenstein, who had lost his family in the Holocaust but had managed to rescue several Jewish actors and to reach the shores of Palestine. There he had slept on a pile of newspapers and had subsisted on a sandwich a day, devoting himself totally and unremittingly to the cause of Yiddish Theatre. Recognizing in Buloff the true artist of his dreams, Gorenstein convinced Joe to return to Israel as an actor and director.

Not only did Buloff return the following season, but he came time and time again for many and varied engagements. Under the management of Gorenstein and later of his partner, Nathan Gilboa, he directed and starred in numerous plays, including *The Kibbitzer*, *The Brothers Ashkenazi*, *The Chekhov Sketchbook*, a double bill of Chayefsky's *Gideon* and *Holiday Song*, *The Diary of Anne Frank*, *The Singer of His Sorrow*, *The Man from Pakistan*, *The Fifth Season*, *Death of a Salesman* and *Tevye and His Seven Daughters*.

The standard procedure for the producer was to engage Buloff for a season and to send him the airfare; Buloff would arrive with a script or scripts and would audition local actors to assign parts. If he felt he needed a specific actor for a role, he would often draw on the well-known Hebrew-language Habimah Theatre. After rehearsing his cast for four weeks, he would open at the Ohel Theatre in Tel-Aviv and thereafter the company would take the play—with sets, costumes, etc.—on a tour to Haifa, Jerusalem, and almost every town, village and kibbutz in the land. Such was the general practice in Israel (and sometime still is), whereby, instead of the audience coming to the play, the play comes to the audience.

Uprooted by war and the Holocaust, most surviving European Yiddish actors had come to Israel. Under Buloff, they gained direction, both self-respect and the respect of the public, and inspiration. For Joseph himself, his work in Israel constituted the realization of a lifelong goal—to bring back to life the tradition and style of his old Vilna Troupe for audiences that understood and loved Yiddish.

When our daughter, Barbara, grew old enough to travel, she and I began accompanying Joe to Israel, and I played the title role in *The Witch*, (part of *The Chekhov Sketchbook*), and had parts in *Holiday Song* and *The Fifth Season*. My primary function, however, was as an assistant director.

Thus, when we once found ourselves short of funds for our production of *The Brothers Ashkenazi*, I borrowed from our friends at the Habimah costumes from their own earlier productions, had the costumes altered to suit the period of our play, and outfitted our actors so felicitously that the demanding critic Kohansky praised not only the performers but the costuming as well.

Israel's severest art and theatre critic, Chaim Gamzu—who later became curator of the Tel-Aviv Museum—was also expansive in his praise for our production in general and for Buloff in particular.

Years later, Gamzu was incapacitated by a stroke and confined to a wheelchair, turning virtually into a recluse. We arranged one evening for him to be brought to a Buloff recital in the Tel-Aviv Museum, at which Joseph informed the audience that Gamzu was present and paid tribute to his contributions to the cultural life of the nation. The ovation that followed brought tears to Gamzu's eyes. Yet the sharp critic in him did not miss what he referred to as a "jarring Americanism" in a poem by Jacob Glattstein, as he frankly told me the next morning when he telephoned to praise the performance.

We renewed our ties with the painter Reuven Rubin and his wife, Esther. He had designed sets for the Vilna Troupe in Rumania and was now one of Israel's foremost artists. We were also frequent guests in the home of Abraham Meskin, a leading Habimah actor, and his wife, Sima. Our other actor friends included Shimon Finkel, who played our Gideon; Sonia Sheftel, daughter of a Vilna Troupe stage manager, who took over my role as Linda in *Death of a Salesman*; and Lea Schlanger, now a prominent figure in Israeli broadcasting.

On one of our visits to Israel, Joe brought the script of *Mrs. McThing* to show to the actress Hanna Rovina. He was impressed when a young actor, Azaria Rapaport, gave an impromptu reading of the play, translating the English dialogue into fluent Hebrew at first sight. Now Azaria is a diplomat and publicist for his country and has become my dear personal friend.

Playing in Israel meant sharing the perils and anguish of the brave, beleaguered nation. We were touring with *The Kibbitzer* in 1967 when the specter of war darkened the horizon. Our stagehands were called for military duty, and we performed for a while without scenery. Then most of our actors were called into the army, and we had to cancel and return to Tel-Aviv.

War broke out. The American embassy advised all U.S. citizens to return home. "We are staying!" Buloff and I cabled Barbara. "I am proud of you," she cabled back.

We settled down to an anxious wait in blacked-out Tel-Aviv, spending the night in the hotel's cellar shelter, listening to radio bulletins, and expecting an air raid at any moment.

JOSEF BULOFF

Poster announcing performances of I.J. Singer's The Brothers Ashkenazi, starring Joseph Buloff, Tel-Aviv, 1966.

Israeli President Zalman Shazar with Joseph Buloff (in costume) and Luba Kadison, backstage after performance of The Brothers Ashkenazi, *Tel-Aviv, 1966.*

One evening, in the dimly lit hotel lobby, we received a telephone call from our friend Shalom Rosenfeld, editor of *Maariv*. "All is well, Luba," he said, and no more.

"What is well?" I asked.

"Don't ask questions! Just tell Buloff that he will soon be playing *The Kibbitzer* again."

The Six-Day War was won, all of Jerusalem was ours, and within days we were back performing *The Kibbitzer*.

The next war found us in the United States, but its aftermath involved us in a dramatic incident. Right after the 1973 Yom Kippur War, Buloff and I returned to Israel for a recital at the Tel-Aviv Museum's beautiful auditorium as part of the Festival of Israel—an annual event in which we had participated several times.

I was to make the introductory remarks about the writer I.L. Peretz, and Buloff was to follow with a reading of "The Messenger" and other tales. The program struck me as something that Prime Minister Golda Meir, as a staunch supporter of Yiddish literature, would be eager to attend. I telephoned her home, and later received word that Mrs. Meir would indeed attend, but incognito. At the time she was under severe attack, even within her own party, and was reluctant to make public appearances.

The house lights had already been dimmed when we noticed Golda, accompanied by a bodyguard and a friend, slipping into the front row. Buloff proceeded to do his first recitation with extra brio, and, following the ovation, he stepped to the front of the stage and spoke to the audience, heart

Luba Kadison with Israeli Prime Minister Golda Meir, Tel-Aviv, 1973.

to heart. He recalled the primitive conditions under which he had played thirty years earlier on his first visit to Israel, and he contrasted them with the aesthetics and comfort of the modern, air-conditioned concert hall of the Tel-Aviv Museum.

"Look how far we have come!" he said. "And let me tell you, my friends, one of our great leaders who made all this miraculous progress possible is here with us tonight—Prime Minister Golda Meir."

The audience stood up, chanting, "Golda, Golda."

This ovation, started by Buloff's speech, was significant as signalling a symbolic healing of the bitter wounds of the Yom Kippur War.

Backstage, Golda Meir kissed us, hugged us and, with tears in her eyes, thanked us for having set off the demonstration of support for her at a time when she needed it most. That night in Tel-Aviv ranks among the most memorable experiences in our careers.

To this day, in Israel the name Joseph Buloff stands for Yiddish Theatre. He is still fondly remembered by the public, and memorials to him at Beth Hatfutsoth (Museum of the Diaspora) in Tel-Aviv have brought out large, reverential crowds. His semi-autobiographical novel, *Fun Altn Markplats (From the Old Marketplace)*, is being serialized in the original Yiddish by the prestigious quarterly, *Di*

Poster announcing performances of P. Chayefsky's Gideon, *starring Joseph Buloff and Shimon Finkel, Tel-Aviv, 1967.*

Goldene Keit; and it has been published in Hebrew as translated by Joseph Krust. A Joseph Buloff Prize for the best critical writing on the theatre is awarded annually.

An Israeli-born producer in New York City once said, "My father in Israel loved to see Buloff act. He would say, 'Buloff has more expression with his back turned to the audience than most actors have facing front.'"

Cover of Hebrew edition of Joseph Buloff's
From the Old Marketplace, *translated by*
Joseph Krust and published by Zmora,
Bitan-Publishers, Tel-Aviv, 1986.

Book jacket of English edition of Joseph
Buloff's From the Old Marketplace,
translated by Joseph Singer and published
by Harvard University Press in 1991.

The Last of the Vilna Troupe

Having started this informal memoir with the boyhood of my father, it seems appropriate that I bring it to a close with a few words about his later years.

Leib continued to be active in the Yiddish Theatre in America. He was one of the first directors of the Folkbiene Theatre (still extant as a producer of Yiddish plays), but later moved to Chicago, where he designed sets, posters and advertisements for the company of Julius Adler and Henrietta Jacobson. Known for his versatility in the world of Yiddish Theatre, he was always in demand as a stage manager or as a designer, writer or character actor.

For the Yiddish Art Theatre dramatization of the life of Theodore Herzl, starring Maurice Schwartz, Father executed a brilliant lobby mural showing all the actors in costume. *The Forward* reproduced it in its Sunday rotogravure section.

In the summer off-seasons, he was employed as dramatic director of the Workmen's Circle Camp in upstate New York. Those were his happiest months—when he directed children and mounted charming plays or musicals.

At camp, he formed a friendship with the art director, a young sculptor named Chaim Gross. The two had much in common, for Leib was not only a professional painter but a talented sculptor as well. Never idle for a moment, he would take bits of bread from the table and mold them with his skilled hands into lively figurines of klezmer musicians. I still have several of these miniatures, cast in bronze.

Once, after Gross had attained fame as a sculptor, he recounted with relish a personal story involving his friends the Kadisons, before an audience at the Educational Alliance: He had come to the Kadisons with a delicate question—his romance with pretty young Rena had reached the point where she was insisting that they get married; what should he do?

"What is the problem?" my mother asked. "You love each other, so do it."

"But I have no money," Gross lamented. "I can't even buy the ring."

Whereupon my sister Paula took a gold ring off her finger and handed it to Chaim: "Now you have a ring. Marry the girl, and good luck to both of you!"

Not only did Chaim marry Rena with Paula's ring, but their wedding was celebrated at a dinner cooked by my mother. Afterwards, she handed the newlyweds fifty cents and told them to top the event with a movie.

The marriage of Chaim and Rena Gross was a happy one. Gross remained a lifelong friend of the Kadisons, and he executed a noble bronze bust of Leib.

In 1947, Leib was a stage manager for Maurice Schwartz's company, which was preparing a production of *Noah Pandreh* by Zalman Shneyer. I had a part in the play—that of a madwoman—so once again father and daughter could work together. Just before opening night, I came to the theatre for the dress rehearsal and found my father backstage painting a black piano white.

"Why are you doing that?" I asked. "Can't you get someone else to do it?"

"There's no time," he replied. "Opening night is almost here, and Sam Leve, the set designer, says that for the scene in the countess's boudoir only a white piano will do. It's up to me to make sure that everything is right for opening night."

I looked closely at father and realized that he had aged; he seemed to be dragging his left leg. "But how are you feeling?" I anxiously asked.

"Not bad for sixty-seven," he answered. "But lately I have been suffering from headaches. Also, I have trouble remembering the names of the actors in the cast."

That alarmed me, but I had to put aside my concerns and go on with the rehearsal for *Noah Pandreh*. On opening night, Father collapsed backstage and was rushed to the hospital. The X-rays revealed an inoperable, malignant brain tumor. Six months later, Leib died.

Although Schwartz offered to deliver the eulogy, I chose instead Alexander Azro, co-founder of the Vilna Troupe. He had come upon hard times, had given up his efforts to remain in the theatre and was barely supporting himself and his wife, Sonia Alomis, as a watch repairer. But Azro remained a striking, dignified personality.

Eloquently, he recalled Leib Kadison's leading role in the formation of the Vilna Troupe in war-torn Lithuania, its successful move to Warsaw, and its triumphs throughout Europe. Listening to his recollections, Mother, Paula and I felt pride in and gratitude for Leib's rich, creative life, even as we mourned his untimely death.

My mother went to live with Paula. She never complained, but her gaiety and spirit seemed to have died with her mate. She died twenty years after Leib.

By the 1960's, most of the Vilna Troupe veterans in the United States had died. They had failed to find a place for their talents in the declining Yiddish Theatre, and some had experienced dire need in their final years. But their fate was nonetheless gentler than that of their colleagues who had stayed on in Europe and ended up in the Nazi death camps.

It was in memory of all of them that I undertook a pilgrimage to Vilna in 1986, searching for traces of our past. It was in many ways a futile mission.

The house on Pugulanka Street, where the Troupe was organized and where our actors used to gather, was gone. Vanished too was the marketplace where Joseph Buloff had played and dreamed in his boyhood. I found a Vilna carefully restored from the ravages of German occupation. But not Jewish Vilna. Where once there had been a magnificent central synagogue, surrounded by *shuls* for people of every trade and profession, yeshivas, study halls, now there remained only one humble little *shul*.

Robert Sherman of WQXR, I and other members of our tour spent a Sabbath afternoon there with the aging members of the congregation. We were filled with admiration for the brave survivors of genocide, clinging to their Yiddishkeit in a cold, indifferent city. But we could harbor no illusions that Yiddish Theatre could ever be restored in Vilna.

In Warsaw, I am told, the Yiddish Art Theatre exists only as a sort of museum piece. The once thriving Jewish community of Buenos Aires that used to welcome Jewish theatrical companies from all over the world has been scattered by Peronist and other neo-Fascistic oppression. As for the United States, assimilation has left only enough of an audience for an occasional production in Yiddish.

However, the American theatre from time to time does present Jewish classics in English translation. The YIVO Institute for Jewish Research, founded in Vilna and now established on Fifth Avenue in New York, is one of several societies performing scholarly work in the Yiddish language. There is renewed interest at colleges and universities.

In Israel, there is still hope for a restored Yiddish Art Theater. In 1987, under Mayor Schlomo Lahat's sponsorship, a Yiddish Theatre was started in Tel-Aviv. To it and to all who strive for Yiddish Theatre and culture, I wish success and long years.